C000054329

NOTE TO READERS: THE NAMES OF
CERTAIN INDIVIDUALS DISCUSSED
IN THIS BOOK HAVE BEEN CHANGED.

Manufactured in the United States of America
Library of Congress Cataloging-in-Publication Data
Pimpin' Ken.
The art of human chess: a study guide to winning/
By Pimpin' Ken.
ISBN- 978-0-578-15713-9

1. Life skills – Handbooks, manuals, etc.

1

Pimpin' Ken
Author of
Pimpology: The 48 Laws of the Game published by
Simon & Schuster
presents:
The Art of Human Chess:
A Study Guide to Winning

This book is dedicated to:
My father Collie
"Johnny Slick" Ivy
and
Pimp C

Rest in Paradise
My Family

This book is edited
by:
William Louis Jonathan,
MA Ed

Contents

Preface
Twelve Values One Must Master to
Become a Master Human Chess Player

Chapter One	The Concept of Human Chess
Chapter Two	Tools One Must Use in Human Chess
Chapter Three	Never Underestimate Your Opponent and Always Anticipate His Next Move
Chapter Four	Use Psychology as a Tactic To Get Your Name Out There and to Outshine Your Competition
Chapter Five	Keep a Bag Full of Game: Train Yourself to Out-Deceive Your Opponent
Chapter Six	Plot on Your Opponent with Confusion and Deception
Chapter Seven	Be Hard To Figure Out, Switch Up Often
Chapter Eight	Never Let Your Left Hand Know What Your Right Hand is Doing Because Real Game is Not Transparent
Chapter Nine	Plant Seeds in the Garden of Human Existence and Let Them Grow Long After You Are Gone

Chapter Ten   Use Human Pawns to Do
Your Dirty Work

Chapter Eleven   Always Show Strength
When Necessary Playing
Human Chess

Chapter Twelve   `Make a Grand Appearance
and Shine at All Costs

Chapter Thirteen   Master the Art of Keeping
Top Flight Status and
a Good Reputation

Chapter Fourteen   Make the Prize
Worth the Chase

Chapter Fifteen   The Various Arts One Must
Employ to be Great at
Human Chess

Chapter Sixteen   The Methods and Tactics
I Used To Get in Good Grace
with the Celebrities

Chapter Seventeen People That I Personally
Know As Human
Chess Players

Chapter Eighteen   The Greatest Human Chess
Players Of All Time

Final Note

Preface

"Without a roadmap or navigation system, you will get lost."

~Excerpt from:
Pimpin' Ken and Karen Hunter
Pimpology/The 48 Laws of the Game
Published by Simon & Schuster~

*"In theory, there is no difference between theory and practice.
But in practice, there is."*
~Yogi Berra~

Life is like a chessboard and we are all human chess pieces. What determines where you are on the chessboard of life is your ability to strategize, deceive, plot, plan and maneuver. Over and over again, we hear the axioms, "I play chess not checkers; This is chess, man; Let your next move be your best move." But what do these sayings really mean? In this book, I will break the game of chess down and add a human element to it. I have written it in a way that a baby could understand but a genius may be baffled.

My purpose is to construct the street version of Robert Greene's book *The 48 Laws of Power* or Sun Tzu's *The Art of War*. However, you will find it to be just as profound, minus the intellectualism. If you have ever been to Five Points in downtown Atlanta, you may have witnessed the many people playing chess. These men are focused on their games like a laser beam. They have to be because chess is based on strategy. You must deceive and maneuver around your opponent as well as simultaneously plot and plan your next move. Ironically, these are the attributes we use in our everyday human affairs. In the hood, we have one name for this: Game. Most street dudes use these tools everyday as they run their con games, pimp their girls and sell their drugs. If they only knew that some of the richest tycoons, politicians and entertainers use the same principles to make millions without committing crimes.

My aim is to show the contrast between the two worlds and merge them, creating a universal principle called human chess. This principle will empower men and women and give them the necessary tools to find strength within themselves so that they may reach the potential of their destiny. All humans were created to be powerful beings capable of achieving any goal within the resources available to man.

The questions with any great thinker when pondering another's success are, "How did he make so much money? How did she become so powerful? How did he turn into the most influential man of our time?" I will break down and decode the strategies and maneuvers that Jay-Z, Dr. Dre and 50 Cent used and dissect the reasons they have been, are and will continue to be on top. I will show you how Obama got to the White House using game and by mastering the art of human chess as described in this book. I will take you into the cold world of the streets and show you how deception is a must. Even if you are not the type of person that plots and schemes, your enemies are always plotting on you. This is why strategies and planning are essential to survive in the game.

There is very little difference between a stockbroker and a petty conman on the streets. They both lie for a living. One lies for millions and the other lies for thousands. What I do in this book is give you live examples of the game and the principle and call it *The Art of Human Chess*. By doing so, I hope I can bridge that gap and let the world see we all speak the same language and the name for that language is Game.

I've been in the game for thirty-five years and I've done it from the ghetto streets to the executive suites. I ran game on dudes in the streets and took their girls and money and sent them on missions. The funny thing about it is the largest amount of money I have ever made at one time was in the executive suites. It made no difference what field I was in, the streets or the suites, I had to be a master human chess player. In the streets, I ran game. In the corporate suites I used the principle of human chess laid out in this book.

For those of you that are already human chess players, this book will serve as confirmation to you and you will say to yourself, "I've been doing this my whole life." Those of you who find it offensive will come on board in theory, but will convince yourselves that you are a good boy or girl and you would never deceive, trick or outfox anyone. But that's where you don't understand the principle as being not that of a tyrant, but as someone who is hungry and wants and needs to live.

We as human beings are born with deception. For example,

when my two sons, 'Lil Kenny and Supreme, were babies, they would cry every time they were hungry, needed their diaper changed or wanted to be picked up. I would be watching a Lakers game and Preme would look at me as if he was saying, "Dad, come pick me up." Of course, I'm into the game so I'm not going to pick up a baby. He plots in his mind, "I have to get Dad's attention," and out of nowhere, he starts to cry–Game. I know I'm into the basketball game, but I pick him up to stop the crying. 'Lil Kenny sees me picking up Preme and gets jealous and he starts crying. Being a master of the game, I know that I'm being deceived by my boys and it only came natural to them because we are human. You get the point?

What this book is going to do is give you an upper hand in the game and make you a master at human chess. Let me point out to you how this works by showing you some of the chess moves I exercised that helped me to get where I am, and you will see that we are the same or that perhaps you have been a victim of some of the traps, plots or game by people like myself. Being a master of human chess, I would always plan and plot my moves ten to twenty steps ahead. In other words, I would predict the outcome of all my situations. I used deception to throw off my opponents and gain leverage. This allowed me to maneuver and set traps.

My first strategy, as I pointed out in my first book *Pimpology: The 48 Laws of the Game*, was to build a name for myself. I realized that most people are fanatical and it is easier to sell a Coca-Cola than a regular cola. The reason is because of the branding and marketing strategies that the larger corporations have used to manipulate the mind into thinking that these products are better. So I had to build my brand to the point that I was able to attract A-List entertainers. This should not be surprising because the larger brands like Nike, Coca-Cola and Chrysler do it all the time. The difference between them and me is they have the bankroll and I have game.

Once I devised a strategy on how to get people that would normally receive millions from these corporations to do the same thing that they do for me for free, I knew it was a wrap. It was a clever tactical maneuver because all I did was went to the artists' friends in the hood and sold all of them DVDs. Now their friends are my fans which made it a must for the entertainer to know me.

There was only one way to prove that these entertainers knew me and that was to put me on their platinum albums that were about to be released. If you Google my name right now, you will see that there have been over fifteen million albums sold featuring me and I didn't pay a dime. I played human chess and plotted my way into the entertainment world. It would have cost me millions in advertising if I would have paid for it.

In essence, you have to be able to identify game when you see it. Once you understand it, you will be able to better control your situations and make money in more ways than you could imagine. This secret is not to be played with once you learn how to plot, plan, strategize, maneuver and exercise extreme patience. You have to stay on your game. Excellent chess players always attract competition because your moves are so clever that people feel they need to bring you down. These are called haters and they are your opponents. Your only defense against them is to read and re-read this book until you master this principle called human chess, which in the streets we call game.

This book will serve as your study guide and I suggest you take notes. I have included a note page in the back of each chapter. Good luck and remember the whole world plays human chess and your job is to not get checkmated.

Twelve Values One Must Master to Become a Master Human Chess Player

- ❖ **A positive attitude:** You must unequivocally and positively look at the world as something good and a place where you can win.
- ❖ **A desire to win:** Desire is the cornerstone to all achievement. If you have no fire in you, it is hard to see yourself as a success.
- ❖ **Persistence:** This could be a book within itself called *The Art of Never Giving Up*. Pursue your dreams until you have nothing left in you.
- ❖ **Imagination:** You must have the ability to see things in your mind and to wonder about things that have not yet come to pass.
- ❖ **Self-confidence:** Believing in yourself is a must to be a good human chess player.
- ❖ **Conquer fear:** President Kennedy once said, "The only thing we have to fear is fear itself." You can never play the game of human chess and fear your opponent.
- ❖ **Patience:** Knowing when to make the right move and taking your time to do so is key to crushing your opponent.
- ❖ **Plot:** Thinking and setting up all of your moves and out-thinking your opponent is a must.
- ❖ **Strategize:** Have a strategy if you want to win in any game.
- ❖ **Manipulate:** Don't think of this as a negative. Often we hear businessmen and government officials say, "We have to manipulate the situation." This simply means make it work for them.
- ❖ **Deception:** If people know your game plan they will destroy

you. Deception throws them off and leads them astray.

❖ **Tolerance:** You have to be able to accept others' differences and experiences to be a master human chess player.

Read these principles twice daily until you have mastered them. You may not master them the first time around but do not be discouraged. Stay on course and these principles will become law in your daily life.

Chapter One
The Concept of Human Chess

"Every game has rules, and you'd be crazy to think you can come into them without knowing them."

~Excerpt from:
Pimpin' Ken and Karen Hunter
Pimpology/The 48 Laws of the Game
Published by Simon & Schuster~

*"Try to learn something about everything
and everything about something."*
~Thomas Henry Huxley~

The concept of human chess came to me by way of an OG I met while I was serving a bid in Oxford Federal Penitentiary. I was young and thirsty for game. I had read *The Prince* by Machiavelli, *Think and Grow Rich* by Napoleon Hill and the *Art of War* by Sun Tzu, so I was somewhat abreast with the mind games that people play. The only thing I was not up on was chess as a board game. I was always hearing veteran players say, "Life is like chess," and, "I play chess while these suckers play checkers." I heard a lot of references to the game, but never knew how profound the game of chess really was.

One day I was in the prison yard and I walked up to these two OGs playing chess. One of them was an ex-pimp turned bank robber and I said, "I see two masterminds at work." I said it like that to make them feel some type of way, like bosses. And the one I wanted to pull my coat looked up and said, "Boy, what you know about this shit right here?"

I replied, "Nothing."

"Nothing? Youngen, you're slipping. All boss players play chess. It's like life and the more you play, the sharper your game will be."

Now he really had my attention because there was nothing I wanted more than to be a boss player. I scrambled my brain for a slick way to hit on him for that chess game. I asked, "Are you the truth or are you just going through the motions?"

"Nigga you haven't heard? I'm the best in this whole motha fuckin joint. I've been in here for fifteen years and I run circles around these lames when it comes to this shit right here," he replied, pointing at the chessboard.

I asked him, "If that's true, then you can teach a young pimp the game, right?"

He looked up and said, "Man, you're smooth and I like your game. So yeah, let me checkmate this dude and it's on." He checkmated him and I sat down, and the long session began.

The OG said, "First let me say, I'm going to put this shit in terms you can understand. Chess applies to everything and we all live the game of chess. Before I robbed banks, I was a small time local pimp and I played the game the same as I play chess. The Queen is the most powerful piece on the board, just as a bottom bitch is the most important ho in a pimp's stable."

I stopped him and asked, "How does that apply to pimpin'?"

"Well, the main purpose of your bottom ho is to protect the pimp at all times and make sure that the other hos are in pocket. She sets the blueprint for his household. In chess, the Queen moves around and opens up the board so the other pieces can operate better. She sets the stage for how you're going to play the game and takes the opponent's pieces to clear the way for a checkmate down the road. She is your bitch and you depend on her as much as a pimp depends on his bottom bitch. The pawns are like the hos that are there to make your stable look good. If they prove themselves, they can graduate to a big bitch, a Queen. It's the same in the pimp game. You got those bitches that are just down with you and can be taken by another pimp at any time, just like pawns.

"In chess, we players sacrifice pawns all the time, sometimes to trap our opponents. That's why our opponents usually try to wipe out those pawns first. It's the same in the pimp game. A pimp goes at your weak hos first and if he can get them and make you look weak to your bottom bitch, then he goes after her. The knight is like a dirty pimp that snakes a pimp for his ho. It moves sneakily and can trap you when you least expect it. You got to watch the knight like you watch a nigga in the streets. You have dirty pimps that will knock on your hotel room door then turn around and try to knock your ho. They move in all types of ways, you got to watch them. Most good chess players know you got to keep your eye on the knight.

"The bishop is lowdown and loves to lie in the corner and catch you slipping on your rook, who most of the time protects your King. Same in the game, youngen. You got those pimps out there that never come around other pimps, but they're always laying to knock a pimp for his bitch. He is usually the one that gives a pimp that phone call saying, 'I got the bitch.' Now the rook is like a pimp-kicking-it-buddy. It's usually that last piece that gets taken off the board before the checkmate or the pieces that checkmate the other side."

I jumped in and asked, "But how does this apply to us as humans?"

"Young man, what you got to understand is that we humans play chess everyday. For example, the ho deep down doesn't have any respect for herself or the pimp, but she uses the pimp as a scapegoat to make it look like she's being controlled by a force bigger than herself. The funny thing is most pimps think that it's their pimp game that's holding the ho. Women develop five to ten years faster than men and women think way more than men. Men are impulsive and women are analytical, therefore they plot everyday and in everything. Only a master of human chess can outsmart an intelligent woman."

I interrupt, "Ok, what are you saying? Is a ho smarter than a pimp?"

"No, but she is going to try her best to break a pimp down. It's in her nature to break a man down and a pimp is a man. In the Bible, the first thing you read about is the fall of man. Eve broke Adam's ass down. That story was about how to play life's game of chess and Eve checkmated the shit out of Adam. A ho plays on tricks all day and if a pimp is not on his game, she will try him too. That's why pimps that understand this tell a ho to wash the trick off of her before she comes home to psychologically separate herself from the trick. He plays mind games with her so she never sees him as a trick or a buster."

"Good shit, OG. How does this chess shit apply to the pimps?"

"Pimps play chess with one another all the time. Why? Because it's a game of competition. I want your spot, your ho and better shit, so I set traps for you. I use deception and manipulation. I will lay low to take your ho. These are all tools used in chess. A wise pimp will always keep his guard up and never trust another pimp.

Play chess or checkers, play or get played."

"What about if a pimp has more than one ho?"

"He has to master them all and make them feel like they are all the same, even though there will always be one that he trusts more. He's going to have to make it where he's the only prize and that they are all lucky to be under his instruction. It's all chess and finesse."

"Ok, what about a pimp's character?"

"This is what it's all about. Every master of the game knows that a campaign is everything. Like in chess, a pimp must be feared and respected or he will be attacked from all angles."

We stopped talking and began playing. After a few games, I was able to see how the game of chess applied to everyday life.

THE BREAKDOWN

My critics say that I'm cold-hearted, manipulative, conning and deceptive. They feel this way because they never have to deal with these sharks and lions that I deal with on a daily. These motha fuckas are constantly trying to bite my head off and tear into my flesh. Sometimes I'm as manipulative and conning as a lion and sometimes I'm as cold-hearted and deceptive as a shark. It all depends on where I'm fighting. If I'm in the water and I'm fighting a lion, I'm a shark. If I'm on land and I'm fighting a shark, I'm a lion. Just know that I fight to win and in the words of Malcolm X, "By any means necessary."

This shit is human chess and I'm trying to win at all costs. The OG taught me the game and I took it and ran with it. The only difference between him and me is that I'm out here in these cold-hearted streets where you have to be on point at all times. There are many human chess players that live by certain codes that will eat you like meat and spit out your bones. They practice deceit all day everyday and lay and play for fresh prey. So I came up with this masterpiece so you can sharpen your game now and thank me later.

You are human so it is impossible for you to escape the many con games and swindles that your fellow human beings use to separate you from your cash, personal belongings and sometimes even your freedom. I've been playing both the game of chess and human chess for years now and by the end of this book, you will be so sharp and up on your game, you're going to log on to www.pimpinken.net and join my game college for some more.

Chess Notes

_____

_____

_____

_____

_____

_____

_____

_____

_____

_____

Chapter Two

Tools One Must Use in Human Chess

"Shit won't happen just because you're sitting around wishing that it would happen. You have to take the first step."

~Excerpt from:
Pimpin' Ken and Karen Hunter
Pimpology/The 48 Laws of the Game
Published by Simon & Schuster~

"When you do the common things in life in an uncommon way, you will command the attention of the world."
~George Washington Carver~

    Tactics: The art or skill of employing available means to accomplish an end; the science and art of disposing and maneuvering forces in combat or a system or mode of procedure. This is a very essential tool in the art of human chess. There are not many moves that are well executed without good tactics. To give you a few examples, when Henry Kissinger used to advise President Richard Nixon, one of the tactics he would use was to give Nixon three choices to make about a certain policy. No matter what choices were given, Nixon always selected the option Kissinger suggested. He understood that Nixon was insecure, so as a clever tactic, he made it so Nixon would believe that he was smart for picking the best option. Kissinger was a masterful human chess player and he knew the right moves to use on President Nixon.

    Another example is the great Magician Houdini who was once challenged by a hater. The hater said that Houdini was using tools to do all his tricks and that any man can do what he did if they had the tools. Houdini accepted the challenge. The stage was set and they agreed to do the trick live in front of a large audience. The trick the hater was going to do was attempt to free himself from some handcuffs. Once he got there, he asked Houdini for the cuffs. Houdini went in the back and checked to see if he had the right code, and he did. Once he was ready, Houdini grabbed the cuffs out of his hands and they started to push each other. As a clever tactic, Houdini switched the code and then gave him the cuffs. The hater tried to free himself and it never worked. Houdini let him think he had the game figured out, but when he was about to make his move, Houdini used a bait and switch move to outfox the hater, a very clever tactic.

    These are the types of things I will show you in *The Art of*

Human Chess: A Study Guide to Winning. I will give you the experience, wisdom and cleverness of some of the greatest human chess players in the world, along with revealing some of their tactics, manipulations and deceptions. Many times I have acted like I wasn't interested in a pretty woman only to end up with her and her mind. This tactic helped me become one of the best to do it and get away with it. If you're going to learn to become a great human chess player, you're going to need great tactics. A wise human chess player always masters excellent tactics because he wants to limit his mistakes and win before he even plays the game.

Deception: The act of making someone believe something that is not true; the act of deceiving someone; an act or statement intended to make people believe something that is not true. For some of us this is against our religion and the Bible tells us that the truth will set you free. When I was a very small child, I would get into all types of shit and my father did not play. Now mind you, I had not yet read *The Art of War* by Sun Tzu nor *The Prince* by Machiavelli, but I would lie like hell to try and get out of those ass whippings. I was trying to deceive my father into believing that he had another kid and that he did it not me. Children are very deceptive. We learn very young how to lie. No matter how religious a society is, it will have to use deception to defend itself. Learn it as an art and you will be a master human chess player.

Maneuvering: A military or naval movement; a procedure or method of working, usually involving expert physical movement; evasive movement or shift of tactics, or a clever management of affairs often using trickery and deception. There is no way you are going to master human chess without understanding how to maneuver. The first thing I learned in the entertainment business is how to move and win stars over. I would get what I want and move to the next star. This is what Jay-Z, Puff Daddy and all the vets do. They lay for a new artist to get a hit and they get on the remix. This is clever maneuvering because they get access to the new artist's fan base and this continues to make them relevant. You will see this a lot in this book, so master this art.

Plotting: A person who secretly plans to do something. This is when you set traps and have others collect info on your opponents and they don't even know it. When I was young, I lived in an environment where people plotted all the time, so I had to counterplot and make sure I never got caught in their traps. This is a good skill to master because it works two ways. It keeps you from getting played and it helps you when you are playing. This book will show you some of the best plots ever executed and help you to become a master at plotting.

Patience: Ability to remain calm and not become annoyed when waiting for a long time or when dealing with problems or difficult people; done in a careful way over a long period of time without hurrying. This is an art and virtue that you must master in order to become a master at human chess. The person that takes his or her time and waits to make the best move will win the game ninety percent of the time. A patient man is a wise man.

Plans: A set of actions that have been thought of as a way to do or achieve something; something that a person intends to do. My favorite sayings are, "A man that fails to plan, plans to fail," and "You must plan your work and work your plan." Planning is something we all must do. What a plan really does is gives you a blueprint and a road map to get you to your goals in life. Human chess players never leave the house without a plan. You can't win without one.

Strategy: A careful plan or method for achieving a particular goal usually over a long period of time; the skill of making or carrying out plans to achieve a goal. Every military general devises a strategy before he goes to war and if you're going to master human chess, you must to the same. To write this book, I had to put together a strategy. I wanted to be sure that I reach the educated as well as the everyday person.

Always have a strategy and you will win the majority of the time. These tools are going to be very helpful in shaping you to become a master human chess player. You will understand why you need to plan, plot and be patient. Your maneuvering and clever deception will help you outfox your opponents. But it will be the strategies you employ that will determine whether you are a master of the game. If you pay close attention and don't sleep on this boss game, you will learn the secret to becoming a master human chess player.

Chess Notes

Chapter Three

Never Underestimate Your Opponent and Always Anticipate His Next Move

"Wise men know that in order to be ahead of a situation, you must first see the situation in your head."

~Excerpt from:
Pimpin' Ken and Karen Hunter
Pimpology/The 48 Laws of the Game
Published by Simon & Schuster~

"Never interrupt your enemy when he is making a mistake."
~Napoleon Bonaparte~

The game of human chess is a game of deception and manipulation. Your opponent is constantly trying to outthink you and employ the many scams he has in his arsenal of game. You would be foolish to think that he will have mercy if he catches you slipping. Chess is a game of intense focus and anticipation. The man who is good at predicting the other player's moves will be the one who checkmates his opponent in the end. Being paranoid is key. Expect your opponent to be plotting at all times. When he seems weak, train yourself to think it's a trap and he's only trying to set you up for the kill. To underestimate a chess player in human chess can cost you big time.

Years ago when I was in the pimp game, one of the things I did was make sure I kept a bag of deceptive tricks and expected all the pimps to try and take my girls and me to take theirs. I was flashy so wherever I went I was a target and likewise was looking for a target. This kept me sharp and on my game at all times. I traveled all over the country and niggas are different in different cities so I had to have game for everybody.

I was in Washington, D.C. when I pulled up in my turquoise Benz, hit the track and peeped who was who and plotted what nigga I would get first. This young pimp from Portland saw me cruising around the town being fly and decided to befriend me. He gave me a rundown on the town and let me know who he thought was pimping and who was not. He was nice and green so I thought, "This nigga got to be my first target. I will ride with him for a few days then bump him for his hos." He showed me around and let me know what ho was fucking with what pimp and identified the renegades.

I had some fast Milwaukee bitches with me so I put my play into action. I said, "Hey P, why don't you let your hos ride with my bitches and we go sweat these other hos." His green ass agreed. Why did he do that? I called my girls with specific instructions to peel him for his hos and they did just that. In my book, *Pimpology: The 48 Laws of the Game,* I explained that all hos belong to the pimp community and the book on what a ho is going to do has not yet been written. Homeboy was playing checkers and I was playing chess. He underestimated me and never anticipated that I would checkmate him for his hos. I'm the total opposite of what he thought.

After I was there a week, I anticipated that all the pimps would be at my bitches because I was that nigga. I was a boss and everybody wanted to take down the man. It quickly spread that I was fucking with this bitch and that bitch, when the reality was I wasn't fucking with none of the bitches I said I was. The top P's started sweating those hos just like I planned.

I let this go on for two days while I watched in my girl's Lexus 300, a nice but lowkey car. This was a good chess move because now I knew what pimps had it out for me and which ones to checkmate. The pimp that I set my eye on was a tall pretty nigga from New York. I can't say his name because he would kill me if he reads this and knows how I peeled him for his baddest bitch. Like I point out throughout this book, chess is a game of strategy, deception, tactic and manipulation. Once I got the info on his bitch, I quickly deployed my bottom bitch to his bitch's location and told her to say she was thinking about being with a new pimp. I did this so she would let her guard down and underestimate my girl and open up to her.

They worked together for four days and my girl had her ready for the move. My bitch asked her, "Can I use your phone?" Not thinking anything funny, she obliged. My girl called me, hung up and I called her, hung up and she called me back. What we were doing was establishing a call log. This bitch never anticipated the cross. She was slipping big time.

My girl gave her the phone back and said, "Girl, my pimp is tripping. He's talking about he's going to go to your pimp and lie and say you've been on the phone with him. He's going to use our phone calls to prove he called you and you called him. Oh my God, what are you going to do? My man said he's sorry for having so much game, but he had to do what he had to do to cop a ho like you."

She knew she would get killed if she went back to her dude, so she came home with my bottom and I served another nigga for another bitch. This is my past, but I had to show you this graphic example so you can see what happens when you underestimate a master of the game and the importance of anticipating deception, manipulation and the next player's move, because this can cost you.

Another thing I would do when I was in the game was look for girls that were fresh in the game, green and not up on me. Then I would have my Puerto Rican friend (he looks white), Mickey, pull up on the track like he wanted to spend money with her. She would get in the car, he'd give her the money and take her about twenty miles away where I would be waiting. Out of nowhere, Mickey would say, "Bitch, get the fuck out of my car."

I would then pull up on the road where Mickey and I agreed he would drop her off and find her walking alone and say, "Excuse me young lady, are you ok?"

She would look at me with tears in her eyes and say, "No. Can you call a cab for me?"

My response was, "Well, young lady, that would be impossible. Cabs don't run out here."

"Well, could you give me a ride?"

As soon as she got in the car, I would turn my recorder on. This was to assure that she could not lie and say I kidnapped her or tricked her into thinking I was a customer. I replied, "Get in. How did a pretty thing like you end up on such a dark road?"

She appeared relieved and replied, "Oh my god, I don't know what I would do without you. A crazy guy picked me up to spend some money with me. Then out of nowhere, he put me out of his car!"

"So, you are a working girl?"

She hesitated and asked, "Are you a pimp?"

I was on the freeway going farther away from where she needed to go, so I kept it real and said, "Yes, I am. And you are out of pocket. I have you on tape. I know you fuck with Slim the P so you can choose up or let Slim bruise you up. He's gonna put hands on you and I'm trying to put plans on you. If that dude Slim was really about his game, he would have told you to never let a trick take you more than five miles from the track. Don't look confused, baby, choose." I was a nice dresser, very handsome and a master at human chess. She left Slim and ended up down with me. I would use this tactic often. The good thing is that most of the guys I used this on are either out of the game or too old to give a fuck.

THE BREAKDOWN

History is filled with examples of leaders that underestimated the opposition and were ultimately destroyed. One example that comes to mind is Saddam Hussein. He was a man that had a vast empire and one million troops ready to die for him. At one time he was an ally of the United States, but he let power go to his head and attacked one of America's other allies, Kuwait. This was a major mistake on his part. He underestimated the US and didn't think they would go to war for another country. The US did go to war and fucked him up and made him leave Kuwait.

The United States of America is a Superpower and a master at human chess and war. She will set you up for your own destruction and if that doesn't work, here she comes. What happened next Saddam wasn't even ready for and he certainly didn't anticipate the US's next move. President Bush and his Joint Chiefs of Staff said he had weapons of mass destruction (which was later proved to be untrue) and he planned to commit genocide on his own people. They went over there and killed him and destroyed his country. This was a cold chess move on the US's part because it was packaged with deception and a lot of manipulation, which are great tools in the game of human chess. This made the shit I did back in the days look like kid shit.

We can even go back to the days of Cleopatra. She was known for going to war with her siblings and one day they exiled her from Egypt because she was a big problem. Determined to take over, she devised a clever plan. She rolled herself up in a Persian rug and was delivered to Julius Cesar at his feet as the carpet was unrolled. He was impressed and hooked on her. Before it was over, she had him to invade Egypt and restore her back to power and arrest her brother. Back in power, she said, "Fuck Cesar."

Like so many lames and suckers, Julius Cesar underestimated Cleopatra and never anticipated her moves and how she would use him. Always be alert and assume that the person you are dealing with is as clever as me or Cleopatra. Game is an art and the one who plays is very skilled at deception and manipulation. Train your mind to be ready for all game. Then you will be considered a master chess player who is able to peep ten steps ahead and play every opponent like you're playing one of the greatest, Bobby Fischer.

Chess Notes

Chapter Four
Use Psychology as a Tactic to Get Your Name Out There and to Outshine Your Competition

"No one wants to be shown up; it's embarrassing and humiliating, and they will seek revenge. The best rule of thumb is to treat people the way you want to be treated, at least to their faces."

~Excerpt from:
Pimpin' Ken and Karen Hunter
Pimpology/The 48 Laws of the Game
Published by Simon & Schuster~

*"Education is a progressive discovery
of our own ignorance."*
~Will Durant~

Psychology is the cornerstone to this whole human chess philosophy. Understanding the mind and how it works is the key to outfoxing, manipulating and controlling people and your environment. When you are able to master using psychology as a tactic, you will have an edge on your competition.

When I first started building my brand, I knew that I had to use top flight psychology to win people over. I learned years ago that repetition is the best way to reach a person's subconscious mind. So when I got home from prison and in position, I would do parties and promote shows. People thought I was just bringing entertainment to the city. What they didn't know was that I was setting up a vicious takeover using the big name stars as a tactic to repeatedly promote my name with theirs and program the city to know who I am and associate me with all the stars.

This was a nice human chess move, but a better psychological move. I was using the flyers, posters and constant mentioning of my name on the radio as a form of hypnotism. I was tapping into my audience's subconscious minds and they didn't even know it. All they knew was Ken Ivy is the man and he brings all the stars to town. Even the ballers would pay me top dollar to meet these big named stars.

The funny thing is before I devised this master chess move, most of the ballers had more money than me. That didn't last long because I charged $50 for a ticket and anywhere from $100 to $2500 for tables and VIPs. I was exercising boss game and building my name while taking out the competition at the same time. No matter what a nigga was driving or how much dope he was selling, none of those niggas where bigger than me. I used pure psychology to outthink them.

To give you a better example of how this repetition thing works, check this out. Have you ever been in the club and a song came on of a new rapper or singer for the first time and you say, "Who the fuck is that? Put that Jay-Z back on." Then four weeks later, that same song comes on and you change your tune, "That's my shit there! I love that Yo Gotti!" Well, you have been programmed to know the song and like it. The DJ and the record company tapped into your psyche and hypnotized your ass.

I've used this form of psychology in all aspects of my game. In my book *Pimpology: The 48 Laws of the Game,* I talked about when I was in the pimp game and would make my girls write down goals and expectations and read them every day so I could program them. Did you peep how I snuck my book in this conversation? Clever, right? It's all game and psychology and you have to use any and every move to program people. Using this strategy will help you master your skills as a chess player and will assist you in setting up big moves that will be executed later in the game. I used the money from the parties to buy the mink coats, diamonds, a Cadillac, Lexus, Navigator and a big body Benz. By the time I went to Atlanta to work on the stars, they knew me from the shows and I used the money to fit into Atlanta's big baller nightlife.

THE BREAKDOWN

I know that Barack Obama is a clever human chess player and has outwitted those around him to get to the top. But if it wasn't for the media constantly programming the public with his image and message, he would not have had a chance. Obama understood this and he used them to his advantage by getting in the media every chance he could until he became a media sensation. Once the media reached your subconscious mind, getting you to think of the idea of a Black President was not impossible anymore.

This example of repetition by the media forcing the public to accept an individual that previously would have never had a chance to lead the Western world is the essence of the power of psychology and good human chess. All excellent human chess players are master psychologists and know how to get in your mind, to make you believe or do what they want you to do. Learn this and use it at all times.

Chess Notes

_____

_____

_____

_____

_____

_____

_____

_____

_____

Chapter Five
Keep a Bag Full of Game: Train Yourself to Out-Deceive Your Opponent

"No one wants to share their secrets of their game, because they don't want to give another player an advantage. The less your opponent knows, the better."

~Excerpt from:
Pimpin' Ken and Karen Hunter
Pimpology/The 48 Laws of the Game
Published by Simon & Schuster~

"I do not consider it an insult, but rather a compliment to be called an agnostic. I do not pretend to know where many ignorant men are sure – that is all that agnosticism means."
~Clarence Darrow~

Measure your opponents by their actions, not by their words. There is no such thing as honesty or loyalty in the game of human chess. Everyone is out for themselves and they will deceive, lie or do whatever they must to defeat you. So keep a bag of game on deck like some cards. Over the years, I have let some unscrupulous individuals in my life, thinking they were down with me, but all the time they were down to get me.

I remember years ago, I met this dude who seemed to be a real motha fucka, very respectful in the beginning. Saying shit like, "Ken, you a cold motha fucka, man. I ain't never met a nigga like you. All I want is to learn from you so I can have the game, too." I observed the nigga's conversation and it was obvious to me that the nigga was still in the pencil sharpener because his game wasn't quite sharp enough.

I was already a seasoned vet with a lot of game so I was going to peep any weak shit he tried to bring my way. This lame was so sneaky, a motha fucka needed a microscope to peep his ass. I was really trying to see him make it in the game so I was on zero bullshit and didn't need to play him for shit. Come to find out, this nigga was all about deception and backstabbing. He talked behind my back, he stole money from me and he would backdoor me and put chicks up on my game and tell them shit about me. Yes, y'all know I had to serve him with some real human chess. This was a valuable lesson and it taught me to always have a bag of game on deck and not spare any motha fucka.

To give you an example, from that point on whenever I met a fresh chick I would tell her all kinds of shit to keep her off-guard. One of my favorite moves was a Western Union move. This is when you wire yourself some stacks and tell your chick that another girl wired it to you, popularized by Iceberg Slim. This would keep the chick off-guard and make her think you were financially good and that she had some competition. One thing about a woman is that she goes hard when she thinks you don't need her.

Another trick I had in my bag was I would pull out a briefcase full of money, maybe $75K. Count it in front of a chick and ask her, "Baby, can I trust you with all this cash?" The reply was always yes. What she didn't know was as soon as I sent her to get me some water, I switched briefcases and replaced it with one full of fake money. I would give her the briefcase and an address to take the fake money.

You have to know that game recognizes game and a real human chess player is going to always use deception to get the upper hand. I used the briefcase move a lot and luckily for me I never got played by these chicks. But it was all game to see if I could trust them. Fuck, I have trust issues. This was my street shit, but I used it in my business activities as well.

When the daycare business first took off in Milwaukee, I sent a few people to work in the best daycares in the city to learn their system, befriend the parents and ultimately steal their kids. I know, very low down, but this is what human chess is all about and believe me, I'm not the only person on this.

One last example, people used to ask me, "Ken, how did you get two distribution deals and one book deal?" I will put it to you like this. Whenever I would meet with an executive, it would always be in an upscale five-star restaurant. For some reason at midpoint of the meeting, a Barbie-like, professionally dressed chick would walk past us who I would happen to know. I would ask her to join us and she would always oblige. She would order and when her food would come, I would get a phone call.

"Excuse me my friends, I have a 911. Why don't you two get further acquainted while I handle a pressing issue." What I can tell you is that the deals got signed and the executives were very happy.

THE BREAKDOWN

Human chess is a dirty game and most people hate it, especially if they cannot adapt. To become one of the best, you have to go through some shit. You have to have been crossed by a business partner, deceived by a close friend, conned by a stranger or have a girl or boyfriend cheat on you with one of your so-called best friends to understand why game and deception is so necessary in human chess.

I was watching CNN the other day and Congressman Rand Paul said that President Bill Clinton was a "sexual predator" because he "took advantage" of Monica Lewinsky. This was all game to make Hillary look bad and to give him leverage on his bid for the 2016 Presidential campaign.

Deception is everywhere and everyone is on that shit, so you'd better get hip and step your game up. It took me years to get like this and believe me, it's the best thing in the world. There are so many people out here running game, you would be a fool to not beat them to the punch. You don't have to do everybody, but make sure they don't do you either.

Chess Notes

_____

_____

_____

_____

_____

_____

_____

_____

Chapter Six
Plot on Your Opponent with Confusion and Deception

"I may destroy someone, but he'll be okay. He just won't have a career when I'm through. I try my best to put that person out of commission or do them so bad that they don't want anymore."

~Excerpt from:
Pimpin' Ken and Karen Hunter
Pimpology/The 48 Laws of the Game
Published by Simon & Schuster~

"A lie gets halfway around the world before the truth has a chance to get its pants on."
~ *Sir Winston Churchill~*

The fact that I'm writing this book should let you know that I have mastered some of the tricks and trades of human chess. In particular, deception and confusing my opponent are tactics that I use on a regular basis. I learned most of my tricks when I was a very young boy. My father was the best at running game on suckers.

My Pops was from Mississippi and back in the fifties a lot of southern hustlers migrated north to run their con and deception on the so-called city slickers. My daddy and his cousin, Greasy, used to hustle the bars on the west and south sides of Chicago. They would be in the restrooms with their trick dice acting like they were not together. My dad would be the country boy from Mississippi who would make stupid bets like, "Bet I make ten" or "Bet I make four." This would bait the mark in, because with using two dice, ten and four are the hardest points to make. That's when the sucker would open his eyes wide with excitement and say, "Let me get some of that," not knowing he is being deceived by these two country boys. They would take the money and go to the next bar.

He was a master at confusion. He and his cousin used to dress up like assembly workers for GM, wait until lunch break and when the workers would come outside, they would pull out the dice and start playing craps. My dad, being a master at the game, would say, "Bet I make any point on the dice. I feel lucky today."

His cousin would exclaim, "Nigga, who you think you is, black Superman?!"

He would reply, "No sir. I'm just an old country boy from backwoods Mississippi and daddy always told me never be scared of nothing."

Greasy would say, "Boy, you got any money?"

Pops would answer, "Sho' do." He would pull out the

bankroll from his pocket, about $2K. This was deception at its best. Back then, they didn't have casinos and black men would gamble any and everywhere, so the thought of a damn fool talking about he can hit the hardest points in dice would bait anyone. Like master human chess players, they used confusion and deception to trim their victims and in that famous word, checkmated them for that green cash.

One day, my dad said, "Now it's time to show you the game." He told me to get dressed. I did. We got in his convertible Cadillac and headed to the pool hall. While in the car, he began to explain to me his plan of teaching me the game. With his third grade education, he said, "Boy, look here. You got to fool these chumps. Make them think you are the stupidest sucker on this side of the Mississippi. Act like you don't know your asshole from a hole in the front. The dumber you act, the easier they are to trick."

I cut him off and asked, "Suppose they up on game?"

He said, "Most of these niggas out here are lames and all they want to do is take you for your money. Come on, I'm about to show you how the game works."

We pulled up to the pool hall and he reached in the back seat, grabbed his pool stick and we went in. My father, in no time, found his victim.

"Hey man, let's have a friendly game of pool. I'm trying to show my boy the game."

The dude said, "Come on, rack the balls."

They played three games and my dad's opponent won them all. This was the setup. Pops was trying to confuse him and make him think he was the better player. This is how it is in the game of human chess. Sometimes you have to, as Robert Greene says in the book *The 48 Laws of Power,* "Play a sucker to catch a sucker."

My dad said, "Damn, man. You think you're good? Bet $5."

The sucker agreed. For the next four games, he beat my dad. I was saying to myself, "Pops is crazy. He doesn't know what he's doing." Boy was I wrong. He was plotting and the next move my dad did was so classic that it changed my outlook on everything in life from that point on.

Pops pulled out a bankroll that looked like mostly one dollar bills, maybe two twenties and some fives and said, "I'll bet all my money. I got to go."

The fat light skinned dude pull out about $300 and said, "Bet it all then. How much you got?"

"I don't know. We got a bet?" my dad asked him.

"Yeah, bet. We will count it when I'm done beating your ass," the dude said.

He shot and made every ball except two. Now it was Pops turn and he didn't miss a shot. The dude knew he was deceived and it was a trick all along. He was setup to think he could win and this was going to be his big payoff.

He snapped, "Slick ass motha fucka. What you got?"

Pops was slick as fuck. What the guy didn't know was that ten of the dollar bills had hundreds glued on the other side. If my dad had lost, he would pick them up and count them as single dollar bills. If he won, he would flip them on the hundred side. The only way for the sucker to know is if he flipped the bill over and sees the game. Once he picked up the hundred side he asked, "I got a stack here. What you got?"

The dude replied in a meek voice, "You got me," and gave Pops his money.

We got in the Lac and he asked me if I saw the confusion on that nigga face.

I said, "Yeah. He was mad."

My dad smiled, looked at me and said, "See. You got to build them up, confuse them and make them think they got the best game. When the time is right, get their ass."

THE BREAKDOWN

Chess is a game and is played on all levels. Don't think for one second that these large corporations don't use plotting and deception to get what they want. For example, when Wal-Mart wants to buy land to build a store, the first thing they do is buy all the land for sale in the area. Then the city raises the taxes. Now the homeowners have to pay more taxes. Wal-Mart then offers to buy their houses for double the price. Of course they sell, because the taxes are steadily going up. This is deception at its best and the city is always in on the plot. Why? The answer is simple. More jobs and taxes for the city are created when Wal-Mart moves in.

Look at the politics in this country. We can all agree that it is outright nasty. These politicians are masters of confusion and deception, all of them. They leak personal information on one another, spy on each other and work with the media to expose the darkest sides of each other's lives in efforts to bring down their opponent. Life is a ball of deception and confusion and all skilled human chess players know this. So it is wise to learn the game and plot on your next checkmate or be checkmated.

Chess Notes

Chapter Seven
Be Hard to Figure Out,
Switch Up Often

"If you don't get brand new, people will think you fell off. Anyone who stays the same is in a rut, and you have to make changes to stay ahead of the game. You have to keep people wondering what you're going to come up with next."

~Excerpt from:
Pimpin' Ken and Karen Hunter
Pimpology/The 48 Laws of the Game
Published by Simon & Schuster~

*"First they ignore you, then they laugh at you,
then they fight you, then you win."*
~Mahatma Ghandi~

When I was young, active and attractive, the first thing I would do is shake shit up to make motha fuckas uncomfortable. I would pull up in a lowkey whip, scan the perimeter and select my prey. Niggas that knew me would brace themselves because the book on what Ken was going to do was yet to be written. My philosophy is if people know your moves, they will stop you in your tracks and defeat you hands down. When you're slick with it, they'll wrack their brains trying to figure it out.

One of the games pimps play when they first meet hos is to wine and dine them. Tell them all the shit they want to hear, buy them the things they need to work in and make them feel like they're in ho heaven. And luckily for the ho, if she's not with a sophisticated gentleman pimp, these will be her best moments with this pimp. Even though the pimp may be the most hated in the square world, this is a very effective chess move because most prostitutes are cold-hearted. They have to be because tricks or Johns are very manipulative and conning so hos develop a defense mechanism that sometimes makes it home to her pimp. This is why the more skillful pimp switches up before the ho does and becomes the ruling dictator.

That's in the pimp world. But how many of you have met the perfect man, the guy that brings you flowers, opens the doors, tells you sweet things and stays on the phone with you for hours? Or the sexy young lady that's sweet, loves to be around you, laughs at all your non-comedic jokes, and sucks and fucks you at will? Then out of nowhere, shit stops and you wonder what the fuck happened. But you're hooked and you want that old thing back. You want that sweet Ken or Barbie back. This is the power of switch up and being hard to figure out. It leaves the other person confused and wondering what happened to you. Like I said, when I would get to a town or city, I would first come staying off the radar. Then I would pull out the big body Benz, the jewels and terrorize that motha fucka. The advantage was that they didn't see me coming and they couldn't figure me out. I was a human chess player with all types of moves and strategies.

THE BREAKDOWN

It is easy for the reader to say yeah, but how does that apply to me? Well let's start with the Super Bowl. When you see a coach on the field, his main concern is to keep the other side in the dark, not let him read his plays or figure out his strategy. He covers his mouth the entire game just in case the other team has a lip reader. He is a master at chess and his only mission is to outfox his opponent. This requires secrecy and plotting. Whoever wins the game and checkmates their opponent is considered the master thinker. We must be difficult to figure out to win in any game.

Look at Wall Street and corporate America. You can go to jail for inside trading. The corporate meetings are the most secretive meetings in the world because they are dealing with billions of dollars and the last thing they want is the competition figuring out their plans. In all walks of life, you will see this principle being demonstrated. You must master it and become a better human chess player than your opponent.

One last example, in the book *The 48 Laws of Power*, Robert Greene gives an illustration of one of the greatest chess players of all time, Bobby Fischer. Fischer was playing another master at the game that was considered better than him. This guy was Russian and very good at figuring out his opponent's game. Fischer knew this and devised a master plan. He acted like he was unhappy with the arrangements made for the chess match. He didn't agree with the prize money and he claimed to hate the location. All this had the Russian mad as hell and was throwing off his strategy, which is what Fischer wanted.

They finally decided to play and Fischer showed up one minute before game time, increasing the Russian's anger. To make things worse, Fischer basically gave him the first game on purpose. He was making it hard for this master player to figure him out. And to fuck him up even more, he didn't even show up for the second game. Bobby Fischer was playing human chess with this sucker by manipulating his mind and diverting his concentration from the game to Fischer's bullshit. The Russian was trying to figure out what the hell was going on.

By the time Fischer's opponent knew anything, Fischer beat the breaks off of him and that's why he is one of the greatest of all time. He understood the connection between human chess and the game of chess. All games are won in the mind and the player that can keep the other player in the dark will win the vast majority of the time. Live your life, but never let your opponent know how you're living.

Chess Notes

_____

_____

_____

_____

_____

_____

_____

_____

_____

_____

Chapter Eight
Never Let Your Left Hand Know What Your Right Hand is Doing Because Real Game is Not Transparent

"Everybody hates a know-it-all. Even if you do know it all, it's to your advantage to pretend like you don't. If people think you're stupid, they will underestimate you and relax, which gives you the advantage."

~Excerpt from:
**Pimpin' Ken and Karen Hunter
Pimpology/The 48 Laws of the Game
Published by Simon & Schuster~**

*"The only difference between me and
a madman is that I'm not mad."
~Salvador Dali~*

Chess is no doubt a game of finesse and perfect trimming. It is wise and advisable to keep your opponent in the dark and sleeping until you have fully executed your plot and plans. One of the smartest cats I know at this is my man John Devine (JD). When we were shorties, one of our homeboys and I were at JD's crib playing video games and eating junk food. Some time had passed and JD said, "Man, y'all got to go. My mama will be home soon and she's going to tell y'all to leave."

Brandon, our homeboy, very eager to leave, said, "Let's go!"

We left and the next day JD called me asking me about a watch that was missing. I told him, "Call that nigga Brandon and see if he saw it." After a little investigation, JD concluded that the buster Brandon had to take it because he was the only one that used the restroom where the watch was left. Although JD was young, he was a master chess player and wanted to play his cards perfectly so he decided that he was going to play it smooth and not tell Brandon shit. He built him up first and then broke his ass down.

JD began to fuck with Brandon on the regular. He would tell him about all the plugs and made sure he was getting some real paper. Brandon eventually became the man in our hood and was holding some real money. JD, being the master chess player he was and is, finally put his play in motion. He started building homeboy's ego and telling him shit like, "We're family. We're going to rule the game together." This really had this sucker hyped and ready to be checkmated.

JD called an old-school player named Chicago that we knew when we were growing up in the windy city. Chicago was a street nigga that ran petty cons, shot crooked dice, and short-changed niggas, but his specialty was three-card monte. Three-card monte is a game where you have two black cards and one red card. The object of the game is to find the red card. It is mostly played on city busses and subways in major cities. JD organized the move and now he had to bait this lame in smoothly. He called Brandon and said, "What up, P. Let's go to the mall and shop until we drop."

Brandon on the other line asked, "How much should I bring?"

JD replied, "At least 5 stacks. I'm bringing twenty bands just in case they got that new Rolex."

JD used the shopping spree as a smoke screen, because he knew that real game is not transparent and if he told homie they were going to Chicago's crib to gamble, he would peep that and recognize the cross that's about to go down on his monkey ass. JD pulled up in his Benz, Brandon hopped in and JD headed to what seemed like the mall.

Then out of nowhere, JD said, "Damn, man. I got to stop by that fool Chicago's spot to cop those two G's he owes me."

JD knocked on the door and a tall slim gentleman about fifty years old opened the door and exclaimed, "I'll be damned! The rich niggas done came out for some of this ghetto air."

JD, appearing annoyed, said, "Cut the bullshit. Where is my paper?"

Chicago reached in his pocket and was about to hand JD his money, paused for a second and said, "Man, give me a chance to get my money back."

Brandon didn't know, but two masters of the game were at work and he was the sucker ass victim. JD was always on point and very skilled in the art of human chess. He said, "Hell yeah." Chicago pulled out his cards and began to shake the cards and said, "The name of the game is tuck or luck. The more you put down the more you pick up. I don't want y'all to wink, blink or bat your eye because if you do you'll miss your apple pie. I show you this one black and I show you this one red. When you see the red card, point to it."

Chicago gave JD a signal and he pointed to the red card. JD won about three times and Brandon had seen enough. He wanted some of the action. They were playing so well, Brandon wanted to bet his whole five stacks. Chicago and JD were too seasoned to let a mark bet that much, because he might get happy and quit. JD had been waiting for years to get this fuck boy back and being a master in human chess, he knew a good player plans his moves four to five moves ahead. They let Brandon win about three hands at $500 a pop. And the stage was set. It was time for the big payback and JD made his move.

He picked up one of the black cards and threw it across the room, and was like, "Motha fucka," talking to Chicago, "Let's play with only two cards!" When Chicago went to pick up the other black card JD bent the red card as though they were pulling a fast one over on Chicago. Chicago acted dumb like he never saw the bend, picked up the card and said, "If you snooze, you lose. If you chose I sing the blues. If you pick the black it's a sin, but if you win you grin. Show you that they're black and show you that they're red. Who seen the red card? I bet anybody, but a dead body."

Brandon was happier than a nympho with a bag of dicks and his eyes got bigger than fifty-cent pieces. JD pointed to the bent red card and won again. Chicago shouted, "Man! Fuck this! I'm losing all my damn money," and went to a room and came out with a bag of money and said, "Bet big one take little one." It was checkmate time and JD knew he had to play it just right.

JD looked at Brandon and reassured him, "Dog, I got this. I'm going to bet it all."

Brandon yelled in excitement, "Man, what are you talking about? This shit is like taking cake from a baby. I want half the bet."

JD turned to Chicago and said calmly, "Bet it all."

Brandon turned over the bent card and it was black. Chicago counted the paper. It was seventy stacks and he went with them to pick up the money. Chicago took the money and exclaimed, "You niggas ain't slick as me!" and pulled off in his Escalade truck.

JD looked at Brandon and said, "Fuck, man! He peeped me bend that red card."

Brandon replied, "Hell yeah. We lost fair and square."

JD smiled to himself and thought, "Ok, square."

JD is a hell of a human chess player and he only fucks over

who fucks him over. Another case at hand, years ago around 1995, JD took his mother's ring to an Asian jeweler we used to fuck with and this bitch ass motha fucka switched his mom's diamond. Like always, JD didn't get mad he just came up with some real Machiavellian game to checkmate the buster.

JD waited about a week and asked the jeweler if he can make a crown ring and charm. The lame was money hungry so he agreed, even though he knew he had just fucked my man over on the gold and the stones. The stones were straight garbage, maybe some SI 4's, really bad diamonds. JD knew he was about to play this chump way into left field, so he hit him with this, "Hey, I need you to appraise these stones as the best in the market."

He's a greedy motha fucka, so he went for it, "Give me $300 to appraise them." JD smiled because he knew he was playing chess and this bitch was playing checkers. Two weeks later, he called JD and said, "Your shit is ready." JD picked it up, kept it for a week and brought it back and told him to do some more work on it.

A week passed, and the jeweler told JD, "Yo man, I can't find your shit."

JD expected this and replied, "Well, you got to replace it then."

"No problem," the jeweler said.

JD hit him with the checkmate, "Man, you got to replace it exactly like what's on the appraisal.

The jeweler's face turned red, "Hell fucking no!"

JD smiled at him and answered, "You will hear from my lawyer first thing Monday."

I don't know what happened to that jewelry, but JD's lawyer called that Monday and got the number to the jeweler's lawyer. Three months later, JD received $60K in VVS stones. Once again, JD knew how to outsmart a mark and he understood that if they see you coming, it's not game. He kept his mouth closed and never let his right hand know what his left hand was doing. All masters at human chess run circles around simple people because they prefer to play checkers, a game that requires no finesse or serious planning.

THE BREAKDOWN

It's obvious that JD had vendettas to settle. But you have clowns like Bernie Madoff that played for billions and they never saw him coming. He was fucking over doctors, lawyers and very wealthy businessmen and women. Basically, he would take millions from different people at the same time and would send them their own money and make them think they were making a return on their investment.

Like I said, real game is not transparent and even the most devious people can't peep it. Madoff was a mastermind and a hell of a chess player, but somehow he let his right hand know what his left hand was doing and checkmated himself. Hopefully you learned a very good lesson and peeped that if you cross the wrong person, they're going to try and outfox you. The key is to train yourself to read game and follow the strategies laid out in *The Art of Human Chess: A Study Guide to Winning.* Once you know how to peep game, you will enter into all situations with boldness and confidence.

Chess Notes

Chapter Nine
Plant Seeds in the Garden of Human Existence and Let Them Grow Long After You Are Gone

"What is the point in living if no one remembers that you were ever here?"

~Excerpt from:
Pimpin' Ken and Karen Hunter
Pimpology/The 48 Laws of the Game
Published by Simon & Schuster~

"Every day I get up and look through the Forbes list of the richest people in America. If I'm not there, I go to work."
~Robert Orben~

I touched on this subject in my book *Pimpology: The 48 Laws of the Game* in the chapter "Don't Let Your History be a Mystery." Whatever you do, make sure it's a history-making event. When I write books, do DVDs and get on albums, my strategy is to plant seeds that will be here long after I'm gone and my kids and their kids will benefit from my bodies of work. It is a true fact that we are all human beings and no matter what game you're playing, there is another human being playing on the opposite side. We as humans love our sports and competition. The object of this game is to do more than the next person whether it is in scoring or accomplishments.

Look at some of the best athletes in history. Michael Jordan has six rings and broke more records than any basketball player in the game. At the time of writing this book, Floyd Mayweather has been the champ for nineteen years straight with a record of forty-seven wins and zero losses. Muhammad Ali is considered the greatest of all time and is a three time heavyweight champion and he hasn't fought in years.

It's the seeds that they have planted in the garden of human existence that are going to make us remember them as some of the greatest human chess players of all time. These seeds are only going to continue to grow and these athletes/master human chess players will remain the best that did it in their respected fields. I have no choice but to keep building my legacy by continuing to work. This will ensure that the human chess players that come after me will have to raise the bar just that much higher.

To give you an example of what planting seeds can do, many years ago when I was a little boy, my father took me for a ride through downtown Milwaukee and the surrounding areas. He said,

"Son, in thirty to forty years, these neighborhoods will be all whites and the niggas are going to get pushed out and moved farther away from the city."

I looked confused and asked, "Pops, why you say that?"

He looked me in the eyes and said, "Boy, these white people have been raising taxes on all the black businesses and homes around here. They're planting the seeds like good farmers and waiting on them to come to harvest."

My dad only had a third grade education and could hardly read, but I would be damned if the hoods and inner-cities around America don't have luxury condos and expensive apartments, just like he told me when I was a young boy.

THE BREAKDOWN

Planting seeds simply means making moves now that will benefit you at a later date. Those of us who have mastered this strategy benefit immensely from it. Bankers and creditors are best at delayed gratification. They loan you money knowing that they are going to benefit in the future from the loan because of the interest they're going to charge you for borrowing their money. Think long range about your moves like a banker and get the rewards in the end. Plant good seeds and your kids and their kids will eat long after you have moved on. The world will remember you as a great chess player in the art of human chess.

Chess Notes

Chapter Ten
Use Human Pawns to Do Your Dirty Work

"Money doesn't know love. When you're doing business, it's best to put nothing by anyone. People are funny when it comes to money, and trust is a commodity that you just can't afford."

~Excerpt from:
Pimpin' Ken and Karen Hunter
Pimpology/The 48 Laws of the Game
Published by Simon & Schuster~

*"To ensure success, it is best to have the assistance of others
when embarking on a mission."*
~William Louis Jonathan, MA Ed~

There is no way to escape the reality that we are all pawns at some point in our lives. The only thing we can do is recognize game when we see it, but sometimes this can be very difficult. The story I'm about to tell will show you what I'm talking about. Years ago, I was doing a documentary called *Pimpology* and I was going to interview this player named Iceman. He was an older gentleman, much older than me at the time. So I gave him his respect as an OG.

"OG, what's your story?" I asked him.

"Ken, man you pimp hos, but I pimp men and women."

I stopped him, "OG, are you saying you're gay?"

He replied, "Fuck no, nigga. I sell crack cocaine and I got a spot that do ten stacks a day. I have men and women working for me. They're my pawns."

I said, "Cool, tell me more."

"Man, they call me Iceman because I'm a cold-hearted motha fucka. I use any and everybody. I make my workers sit in a caged room for ten hours at a time with a bucket of acid so if 5.O comes through fuckin with my spot, they know to dump the crack in the acid. I force the crackheads to stay after they buy from me because I understand that if I keep them there, they will have to spend all their money with me. Plus they will work on each other to get high. The crackhead hos are my pawns too. I will let them turn tricks in my spot and then make them spend all their money."

"Damn nigga, you use everybody as pawns?"

"That's how you have to be to win in this dirty game. Get the next fool to do your dirty shit and learn their weaknesses and exploit them to the fullest."

"That's some raw shit, but people do it all the time. You're just taking it a bit too far."

He interrupted me, "Man, that ain't shit. I pay my 'lil niggas to shoot up my competition's spot then scream a rival gang just so they can close their spot and go to war. Then I give the crackheads a hit of crack to stand outside their spot and send their customers my way."

I thought for a minute and asked, "Nigga, you not dead?"

He smiled and said, "Nigga, they never saw me. I played the background and let the next motha fucka do my dirty work, using these dumb ass motha fuckas as human pawns."

I said, "Ok. So if they never saw you, how did you get the work down there?"

He laughed and replied, "I got five old ladies I use for that mission. I send them down there to feed the crackheads every eight hours with a bag of groceries. What they didn't know is that I had these soda cans that were really storage cans with tops that screw off. I put the work in the cans with the groceries and give it to the old ladies. They take the food and the dope to the spot and never even knew they were dirty."

I raised my eyebrows and exclaimed, "Wow, nigga! What about the police?"

This nigga went there. "Man, as soon as my spots get to doing good, I call the police on my damn self and leave them about a stack worth of crack and close shop the next day. While they're watching that spot, I start the process all over again at the new spot."

This dude Iceman was a cold-hearted nigga, but he's not the only person that thinks like that. We go about our daily activities not even knowing that we are in someone's spider web being used as live human pawns.

My next example will prove what I just said. There is no argument that young brown, white, yellow and black men are being swallowed whole by the criminal justice system. As a matter of fact, fifty percent of you that will read this have probably already been to jail or are in jail right now. Sorry, but the truth is the truth. Hell, I've been there before myself. It's a system, and unfortunately the system uses our young black men as human pawns. Crime is an easy way out for most young men. The traps that are set to incarcerate these men are so clever that some of our leaders and politicians can't even peep them.

One of the slickest moves that these human chess players did was put drugs in our communities. If you're poor and you see a way to make thousands of dollars in a short period of time, you're going in. So here's what happened. They first let Cuban refugees arrive in crowded boats during the Mariel boatlift crisis. Cubans came to the US and were dropped off in the ghettos of America. They were given tons of cocaine and told to give it to the hustlers. This was around 1984-85. This is the time when dudes started wearing big gold chains and buying nice cars and all that shit. The move was in play. Let them make a lot of money so they can start fighting amongst themselves and begin drugs wars. This was just one of the many moves that came later.

The next move was to bring Hollywood in the picture. You know Hollywood loves money. So they went and got the biggest star they could find to play the part, Al Pacino. That's right. *Scarface* was about a Cuban immigrant who started off as a dishwasher and got a plug on some weight and became this big time drug dealer. Smart chess move, right? But remember, all the Cubans were dropped off in the ghettos of America with all the dope and now this fictional character, Scarface, was a blueprint. Now every dude in the hood wanted to get that Cuban plug.

Hollywood recognized the need for a hood superhero. They were master chess players so they had a meeting and came up with Nino fucking Brown, the brilliant Black head of an organized crime ring who let us know the millions of dollars that can be made from selling crack cocaine. The money started coming in big time. Men as young as sixteen had millions of dollars and they had to protect their money. I was there and I remember all these drug dealers asking everybody to buy them a gun. "I'll give you double the price that you paid for the gun," they would offer. Next thing I knew, people were showing up dead everywhere and the media went to work talking about how drugs were destroying our communities.

What people didn't know was that this was all a part of a larger plan to use these poor kids that never had shit. They began to build prisons and give out stiffer jail sentences so these greedy motha fuckas can make millions off of these ignorant ghetto kids.

Next thing we knew, President Ronald Reagan declared a war on drugs. The government set aside billions of dollars to fight the drug trade. The Black youth in our country were being baited and gobbled up by the system.

So first the drugs, then the movies, then lots of money and of course the guns to protect the money and drugs. You know that the government is only going to let niggas get away with this bullshit for so long before they start locking people up, confiscating everything they've built and putting that money into their own agenda. It's deep, so you have to keep up with me and witness the vicious chess game in play.

Have you ever asked yourself why the former Vice President of the United States, Dick Cheney, owns over $85M in prison stock? It's my opinion that this is not a coincidence, but a plan by the lawmakers to fatten their pockets because, since those Cubans dumped all that cocaine in our communities, over a million people have been incarcerated and hundreds of jails have been built. You can even find prisons on the New York stock exchange and they are doing well. The average sentence given to a man for a drug conviction is ten years, even if it's his first offense. The laws are based on radius of the crime to a school. Therefore, urban areas have stiffer sentences because there are many more schools in urban communities. This means that urbanites or minorities will automatically get more time than those living in rural areas.

Iceman is a bad dude, but he doesn't have shit on the human chess players that create the laws. They make millions of dollars off of these young men, keeping them in jail and working them for next to nothing. Members in the community turn their heads because these guys are really bad and some of them are killers. They destroy our cities and towns, but the truth is they were just pawns in one of the best chess moves ever. The lawyers made money, the judges made money, the jails made money and the families suffer. It's too late to help the pawns that have already been used, but for all the young people out there that read this, put the drugs and guns down. You can't beat the system. They are masters at the game and they will checkmate you with a long prison sentence.

THE BREAKDOWN

As much as this all may sound like a conspiracy, it is true. People are being used as human pawns and the financial rewards for the rich are huge. If you open your mind and really look at this strategy, you will see that the only way people get ahead is by using human pawns. Large corporations are run by maybe ten to twenty top executives that make millions, drive expensive cars and live in mansions while the pawns that work for them drive bullshit cars and pay rent or have a thirty-year mortgage. This seems unfair, but it's America. If you're going to do something big in life, you're going to need human pawns. There is an old saying, "It's ok to use people, but don't misuse people." I pointed out the graphic side of this because most people use this side the most and if you are being used, my book *The Art of Human Chess: A Study Guide to Winning* will give you the knowledge to keep the bullshit off of you.

One last example to young men, the system is real and they are masters at human chess. Please understand that you are a pawn in this game. Right now there is a law called human-trafficking that carries life in prison aimed to lock up any alleged pimp and fill more prison cells. Change your life, get out of the game and do something positive. You may think you're using that young girl as a pawn, but what the system has planned for you will make you a slave and a ho for the rest of your life.

Pimps Up and Hos Down and *American Pimp* was used to trap you into thinking pimping was a way out. It is the same way the movie *Scarface* and *New Jack City* had everyone thinking the crack game was a way out. Look, I was in both of those pimp documentaries and if I would have thought that it was going to make thousands of young black men think that they can use pimping as a way out, I would have told them to kiss my ass and fuck their documentary. If you're not careful, you can be a pawn in a vicious plot. I know you're too smart to be used so keep your pimp head up and think of a better way. Don't let them use us all.

Chess Notes

Chapter Eleven
Always Show Strength When Necessary Playing Human Chess

"It only takes one negative element to ruin all of the hard work of running a smooth operation. You have to prevent negativity from coming in, and if it gets by you, you have to chase it out immediately."

~Excerpt from:
**Pimpin' Ken and Karen Hunter
Pimpology/The 48 Laws of the Game
Published by Simon & Schuster~**

"If you can't get rid of the skeleton in your closet,
you'd best teach it to dance."
~Andrew Marvell~

Your opponents and haters are always watching you and they interpret the way you move. You move one way when you are weak and another when you are strong. You must master your every move when you are playing the game. Even if you have an off day, you must not show any weakness to your opponent. The weak show hesitation and doubt while the strong have an air of confidence and assurance.

Many years ago when I was in prison, I made it my business to never show weakness. It took me about a year but I programmed my mind by telling myself over and over that I was a man and that there wasn't a motha fucka in there that would back me up. I told myself that this is a position I am willing to die for no matter the size of the dude in front of me.

Believe it or not, I became a leader in the joint. I had about fifty cats that would do whatever I told them to do. All of the other bosses in the joint respected me. All the gangs respected me. The COs even respected me because of the strength I exhibited and my unwavering courage.

One day the guard woke me up and said, "Ivy," that's what they do in prison, they call you by your last name, "You are being transferred to Memphis, TN. Get your shit. Let's go." To show that this worked, three weeks after I was in MCI Memphis, a big 6'9" about 300lbs buff black gang member from LA that had life tried to make a move on me. Being a master in the art of human chess as I was and am, I understood that when you're at a disadvantage and weak, you need to appear strong. And as a clever tactic, when you are strong, you have to appear weak to lure you opponent in through his false strength. So here I am like a poodle standing up to a pit-bull.

He said, "Nigga, who the fuck you think you is? I don't know why these niggas show your ass so much love."

I said, "Damn, my nigga! What I do to you?"

He replied, "Nothing. I just don't like you and I don't believe you the nigga everybody thinks you are."

You would have never been able to tell, but I thought I was going to get crushed. O' boy was twice my size and had a life sentence, so he didn't have shit to lose. I'm thinking of a move to throw this big motha fucka off guard. I had been in the joint for three years already and one thing I peeped was that if a convict doesn't have a shank, fights didn't last too long and the prison guard would usually break the fight up in thirty to sixty seconds.

I looked at him and said, "Nigga, fuck you! I'll have your heart delivered to your mama if you think about putting your hands on me!"

I knew I was taking a big risk, but I understood that boldness can create fear in your opponent and that's what I was trying to do in that situation. In the game of human chess, you have to make a bold move to shake up your opponent. You need to make him think about his next move. This also gives the appearance to your opponent that you appear larger than you are.

I guess he thought about it and said to himself, "This little nigga is either crazy or he got some killers trained to go." He grinded his teeth as though he was mad and was going to kick my ass. Then the funniest shit happened. He smiled and said, "Dude, you got a lot of heart."

If you use your mind and strategize your every move, you will be a master in human affairs and find yourself with more victories than losses. I showed strength as a tactical maneuver to ward off a damn fool, but I have also used this in business. For example, when my publisher tried to make me write about some shit I didn't feel was me, I walked out of the meeting and said fuck this book. Yeah, it's true. *Pimpology: The 48 Laws of the Game* almost didn't come out, but thank God I stood up to those corporate lames and didn't show weakness. *Pimpology* is now a classic and inspires so many people in the hood, prisons and even the corporate world.

THE BREAKDOWN

No one respects weakness, only boldness and strength. Back in '96 when I was in Atlanta, the DJ on the radio said, "Ladies and gentlemen, on this day, September 13th, 1996, Tupac has passed away." The chick that was in the car just started crying, almost making me cry, so I asked her, "What's up? You fucked with this nigga before or something?"

I was in the game at the time, so she said, "Naw, daddy. It's just that he was so strong and bold he didn't give a fuck if he didn't like somebody, he was at them."

I thought about what she said and thought, "That 'lil nigga was crazy." He got shot five times and came home riding on the niggas that he thought popped him. He was a 'lil nigga talking big shit to Biggie Smalls and told all of New York fuck them. He had a lot of heart and was bold as hell and this is why he was so loved. When you're a man of courage and you don't back down, it makes you very powerful and larger than life.

Another case at hand was the rapper Curtis "50 Cent" Jackson. You can say what you want about dude, but this dude got shot nine times and did the same thing as Pac, talked shit to his shooters. The only thing about 50 Cent's situation was the dudes he was beefing with were some real killers. 50 demonstrated an act of courage and the people loved him for that. Not to mention, he also went at the biggest nigga in rap at the time, Ja Rule, and did him like David did Goliath.

50 not only showed strength in the streets, but he also proved that he is a strong businessman and now worth hundreds of millions of dollars. Chess is a thinking man's game and all great thinkers knew that the thoughts must be developed by exercising strength and boldness. As a human chess player, never let your opponent see weakness unless it's a set up or a trap to checkmate him. Even if you lose some games, always let them know you will be back to crush them with bold destruction.

One final note, if you are unsure about a decision and you feel unprepared, your best bet is to hold off on making a move until you are in a stronger position. The only way to get rid of fear is to replace it with courage.

Chess Notes

Chapter Twelve
Make a Grand Appearance and Shine At All Costs

"The tighter your look, the greater your potential for advancement. If you're trying to reach the top, you'd better pay attention to details – from your haircut down to the heels of your shoes."

~Excerpt from:
Pimpin' Ken and Karen Hunter
Pimpology/The 48 Laws of the Game
Published by Simon & Schuster~

"If a man does his best, what else is there?"
~General George S. Patton~

Image and style are very important in the game of human chess and most of us judge each other based on appearance. How you look, dress and carry yourself is essential in the execution of your strategies and plans. Jewelry, clothes, cars, hairstyles and physical appearance are tools in the game.

I've been around a lot of masters at the appearance game and the person that impressed me the most was Bishop Don Juan, the big time pimp turned preacher from Chicago. The first time I saw this brother was on Madison and California streets on the west side of Chicago. I was fourteen and had just run away from home. This was where the track was back then and I was staying at this hotel called The Madison Hotel.

I was standing there on the corner with a pimp named Chocolate Dice, a very dark skinned dude who was an up and coming pimp. He said, "There go Don Juan."

I was fourteen, green as a motha fucka and was just a runaway living in a hotel that hos turned tricks out of. I was not in that game yet. In my kid voice, I asked, "Who is that?"

He replied, "That's one of the biggest pimps in Chicago, man. That nigga pimpin' like a motha fucka with his green and gold wearing ass."

I looked at this dude and was amazed at how he commanded respect and everyone was on his dick. I had never seen this man in my life, but at that moment, I became a fan and was hoping one day I would meet him. Don Juan is a master chess player and he has perfected the art of making a grand appearance. This is a strategy in the art of human chess that one must learn and perfect because your first impression has to be your best impression. People usually judge us in the first thirty seconds of meeting us.

Some twenty years later, Bishop and I would do an HBO

special together, *Pimps Up, Hos Down*, videos, parties and press conferences. Everywhere we went, he took the show and like a master chess player, he would take control of the scene. Shining brighter than everyone gave him a big advantage. People wanted his autograph, pictures with him and some people would just stare.

In the book *The 48 Laws of Power,* Robert Greene has a chapter in which he explains if you want to be treated like a King, you have to act and dress like one. Regardless of what people think, to the world Bishop Don Juan is the King of the Pimps. He dresses flashy, wears a lot of shiny jewelry and you can see him coming from miles away. This tactic is powerful because he outshines his competition and is able to checkmate anyone that comes up against him. He is very skillful at this game and I can tell you from personal experience, he's going to steal the show wherever he goes.

THE BREAKDOWN

Bishop Don Juan is just one example. I use him because I had the privilege to work with him twenty years after I first met him. He is indeed a master chess player and has good people skills. Let's look at some of the people that made it in life who were masters at shining brightly. Michael Jackson used his sequin glove, Mr. T. wore fifty gold chains, Marilyn Monroe was famous for her blond hair and Don King styles his hair to resemble a crown. Each person had something that was their signature that the world associated with them and would try and emulate.

When you're playing human chess, you have to give yourself an advantage. Making a grand appearance and shining by any means necessary is key. It forces your opponent to fall back and peep the show you're putting on. Even in the business world, the CEOs that are well groomed and wear the tailored suits are the ones that make the most money and get the most respect.

Study these great attention-getters. I did. This is why when you look at my pictures on Instagram @realpimpken, you see me wearing a thirty carat diamond pinky crown, custom minks and a top dollar sprayed Rolex. I drove the $200K cars so people would say, "There he goes." My opponents in human chess, the haters, only hate more. When I deal with corporate America, I put on the Italian shoes, the Armani suits and a Yacht-Master conservative Rolex, playing the part fit for the script, but all the while shining and making that grand appearance.

Chess Notes

Chapter Thirteen
Master the Art of Keeping Top Flight Status and a Good Reputation

"Do things in a way that people want to follow your lead. Don't be a follower. Don't ask, 'What happened?' make shit happen."

~Excerpt from:
Pimpin' Ken and Karen Hunter
Pimpology/The 48 Laws of the Game
Published by Simon & Schuster~

"When people show you who they are, believe them."
~Maya Angelou~

Over the years, I have heard of a lot of cats with boss street status such as John Gotti (New York), Al Capone (Chicago), Nicky Barns (New York), Frank Lucas (Harlem), Jim Dandy (Milwaukee), Fluky Stokes (Chicago), Michael Conception (Los Angeles), Pee-Wee Kirkland (New York) and the list goes on. Whatever these dudes did in their lives, their reputations have remained intact in prison and on the streets. Don't get it twisted, I know the list is way longer than what I just wrote, but my point is that these guys were master chess players because they just kept getting larger and larger. A good chess player plays by certain rules and he stays true to them until the end. This is how one keeps his status.

When I was young and first went to Wales (a juvenile detention center in Wisconsin), I made up my mind to establish a solid reputation. I didn't play with niggas, didn't talk to niggas and if someone wanted to fight me, it was on. One day this dude named Tony walked up to me and said, "Boy, you know I'm a knockout artist, don't you?"

I looked at him and asked, "Why the fuck is you telling me?"

He smiled and said, "You a little tough nigga, huh?"

I said to myself, "I hope dude moves around, but of he don't, it's on."

Now, Tony was that dude for real. He had put to sleep about ten niggas in Wales. I knew I had to stand my ground if I was going to get any status around that joint and I did. The next day the word got out that I stood on Tony and wouldn't let him get the best of me. He was mad, so he came over to my unit with this bully nigga named Carl. I was playing pool and acted like I didn't see them. I was young, but my mind was always operating like a chess player. I was planning my moves before they got to me. Tony swung, I weaved back and hit him. Then I got at Carl, totally fucked them up with that move. Next thing I knew, pool balls were scattered everywhere. After that fight, my reputation was established in the joint.

Thereafter, I ended up in the big prison (Green Bay Correctional Institution) and then ultimately in the Feds. And no matter where I went, I had status and a good reputation. One thing about status when you're a human chess player is that it makes it much more difficult for your opponent because he knows you're a boss and you're not going to lie down without a good fight. Because I'm a master at human chess, I make it my business not to give a fuck about who the opponent is or his status. I want to crush him and thinking about what he did or how he did it won't cut it.

Now the flipside to that is I'm going to use whatever is at my disposal to outwit him. My status is first and foremost. I built the brand Pimpin' Ken so niggas know what it is when I step in the building. Pimp C (RIP), Puffy, 50 Cent, Nelly, 'Lil Jon, Too $hort, 'Lil Wayne and the whole rap game respect me. I've chilled with all of them and they have millions of fans and still respect Pimpin' Ken.

Why am I saying this? Because I want you to see why I can make the moves I make. By me building a relationship with these powerful dudes, my status shot to ten. This gave me an advantage over any player who got in my business. I was able to get in magazines, on the radio, TV shows, etc., all because of who I was and my status. I haven't been to prison in twenty-five years, but they respect me in there like they respect all the OGs. I talked at the beginning of this chapter about who has maintained a good name in this game and top flight status. Shit, my book is outselling all the urban books in the joint. They love me in there. Checkmate.

THE BREAKDOWN

Your status is like a double-edged sword. It can cut going in and coming out. Some people will always respect who you are and know not to cross you, but there will always be those haters that will spend a lifetime trying to get at you on some bullshit. So stay focused and treat everyone like they're out of pocket. Sometimes you have to play the fox and outfox your opponent, a master chess move. Let them get at you then fall back and make them look like the hater to the public and watch public opinion turn on their ass. Their reputation will be in question, not yours. Most masters at human chess know that a good reputation will precede itself and the wise know not to disrespect a master's reputation. Only a fool would challenge a master of the game and he's not qualified to even shine a master's shoes.

Chess Notes

Chapter Fourteen
Make the Prize
Worth the Chase

"What looks like a bargain may be more than you bargained for, and if something looks too good to be true, it usually is."

~Excerpt from:
Pimpin' Ken and Karen Hunter
Pimpology/The 48 Laws of the Game
Published by Simon & Schuster~

"The artist is nothing without the gift,
but the gift is nothing without work."
~Emile Zola~

As a human chess player, it's important that you assess the value of all your moves and don't make any uncalculated moves just to make a move. When I was in the game, I didn't try to steal just any chick from any dude. I would pick the chicks that were with the biggest pimps and had the biggest hoing.

One day, a fellow pimp and I were riding and he said to me, "Ken, I like what likes me. I don't have a precedence when it come to a ho as long as she got some dough."

I replied, "Yeah, I feel you, but as you get more degrees in this game and you start playing chess and not checkers, you begin to pick your hos like a farmer picks his fruits, ripe as a motha fucka."

What a lot of upstarts in this game don't understand is that his present choices will determine his future happiness. I want to knock a chick that everybody's talking about so when I cop her, it will make the daily pimp news. I want a chick that fucks with the biggest player out there because this means that my game is tighter than his and it's going to put a cramp in his style, which may make his other girls curious enough to fuck with me too. It's like going to war. You want to win the war before you go. This makes the prize worth the chase and you kill a lot of birds with one stone.

He said, "Man, that's ho discrimination. I may have to report you to the NPA (National Pimp Association)."

I grinned, "Man, those motha fuckas on Wall Street got the game on lock. They study the stock market all day and pick the most profitable stocks to invest in. Pimpin' is big business and a pimp has to be wise in his choices because hos are up and down just like stock."

He said, "Yeah I can dig that, but they all the same to me. Money, money and more money."

I schooled him, "That's why you're still trying to be the man out here because you made some bad choices. Think before you act and pick the best the first time around and you won't have to keep wasting your time. Time is money and make sure whatever you do is worth your time. Choose quality over quantity. One bad bitch is worth more than ten funky hos."

I dropped him off and thought to myself, "Life is short and we're only here for a brief time. It is always wise to only do shit that's beneficial for you."

THE BREAKDOWN

When I was in prison, I used to watch the masters at the game of chess play in the yard. These guys never played anything but the best and if you weren't labeled as a master around the prison, forget it. They would never play you.

One day I was in the prison library and I bumped into one of the prison chess masters and I said, "Yo, my dude. Why you niggas be acting funny with that chess shit?"

He replied, "No, P, it's not like that. Any motha fucka can play if he qualifies. Chess is a thinking man's game and the better your opponent thinks, the bigger the prize and the more points you get in the chess circles. We just want the prize to be worth the chase."

This was some real game. I took it to heart and applied it to all aspects of my life. When I'm playing human chess, I want to be sure I'm going to not only win, but get something out of it. So I choose not to touch anything that doesn't turn into gold.

A dude I know that's a local Milwaukee rapper said, "Ken I'm playing chess with these niggas. I'm going to be the best rapper this town has ever seen."

I smiled and said, "Nigga, you're playing checkers. If Jay-Z, 50 Cent, Yo Gotti, Drake or 'Lil Wayne is not your competition, the prize is not worth the chase. Aim for the moon, even if you don't get there you will be amongst the stars."

Chess Notes

Chapter Fifteen
The Various Arts One Must Employ To Be Great At Human Chess

"In business you have to exploit every situation you can – if friendships prevent it, then you are not on even footing with your competition, and you will lose."

~Excerpt from:
Pimpin' Ken and Karen Hunter
Pimpology/The 48 Laws of the Game
Published by Simon & Schuster~

*"The supreme art of war is to subtle the
enemy without fighting."*
~Sun Tzu~

The Art of Psychological Warfare

When you see the President of the United States going to a meeting, more than likely he will be wearing a red or blue tie. The reason is because these colors represent power. To give you an example, when I first attended my meeting with the publishing company Simon & Schuster that published my book *Pimpology: The 48 Laws of the Game*, I wore a light green suit and all my jewelry looking like a straight clown. I did this because I wanted to see how they were going to view me. I can assure you that they thought I was a joke.

The next time I met with Simon & Schuster, I wore a dark blue Armani suit with a dark red tie. They treated me like a businessman. It's all psychological and you have to play mind games in human chess. If I didn't let them know I knew how to speak well and dress accordingly, they would have had no respect for my ideas. The purpose is to give your opponent something to think about and to see you as a clever mastermind.

A famous friend of mine I'll call T was disrespected by another famous person. T felt offended because this person had a lot of influence and speaking bad about my friend could make people take sides and at that time, he was a larger star than my friend. T could have had a war of words, but he wanted to make this guy really feel him. He wanted him to know that he was nothing to play with, so the psychological war was on. He had his manager call the other famous person's manager and book him for a show. It cost $40K to book him. They agreed on the price. My dude's manager sent him the deposit of $20K and faxed over the contract. Thirty days later, he flew to where the show was to be held. The limo picked him and his boys up at the airport. While they were in the limo, T called the other dude from a cell phone and said, "Player, it's not nice to talk slick to a boss. I can touch you at any time. Please keep my name out of your mouth."

Dude jumped out of the car and told his boys, "It's a set up!"

T was one car behind peeping the reaction and said, "Dude ran to the police." The police couldn't do shit because there was no crime committed. T didn't want to kill him. He just wanted to fuck his head up mentally. Just the thought that he could have been dead was powerful enough to make dude keep his mouth shut and keep T's name off his lips.

My father used to always say, "Gambling is 80% psychological." For example, my father would bet on the worst team in basketball. He would say, "Bet $300 the Wizards beat the Heat." And every time the person would take the bet. My father would then leave and tell the victim (vic) to call him when the game was over. And just like he planned, he would get a call from the vic who obviously thought my father was a damn fool.

My father would then tell him, "Meet me at the bar," which was my uncle Greasy's bar, "so I can pay you." My dad would pay his $300 bet and then pull out his dice and say, "Let's play. What they hit for?" The vic always took the bait and pulled out the money my dad gave him and some of his own. He would walk away broke and my father would have all the money. The psychology behind what my pops did was he played a fool to catch a fool. He made him think that he was a lame only to wipe him out with game. Human chess is real and if you sleep on it, you will come up short every time.

I once read that Queen Elizabeth, the virgin Queen, would flirt with every King from the surrounding countries making them think that she might marry them, therefore leaving them under the hopes that they would acquire her kingdom. A marriage with the Queen meant more power. The Queen was clever and she played with all of their minds and had them kissing her ass. They competed for her attention, gave her all kinds of gifts and she never married any of them. Her nation had no wars and she died a virgin Queen. The Queen used psychological warfare to outsmart her enemies and watch them kill each other trying to impress her while she enjoyed years of peace.

My brother and I were talking once about how the CIA used sleep deprivation and water boarding to get information out of people. These mind games are for real because the person that receives the punishment really thinks he's going to die. When the CIA uses water-boarding, they put a bag over their heads and pour water all over their face. This is powerful because it makes them think they won't survive the water and they are going to drown. When they were using the sleep deprivation tactic, the CIA would play loud music all night so their detainee couldn't sleep. This would drive them crazy to the point where they would do anything just to get some rest.

Psychological warfare is very necessary in human chess. You must get in the mind because if you conquer the mind, the body will follow. The best players of this game are the political leaders of this country. Look at the senators and congressmen, they look like weak old men that wouldn't hurt a fly, but disrespect them or this country and you will see them transform into straight killers. They will kill an enemy as fast as you can blink an eye. They look humble and clean shaven just to make it look like they're harmless so they can do business without instilling fear. But I can assure you that their look is psychological. Behind that look is a cold human chess player that will do anything to win and checkmate your ass. They have control and they're not going to give it up. You go against the US and you are going to lose.

The man or woman that masters this art is at an advantage. He or she doesn't get caught up in people's traps because they know that from a psychological perspective, it's best not to chase a person if they start to act funny. The best defense is to withdraw and let them know you are in control. It's a part of human nature to kick someone when they are down. Play mind games and make your opponent feel that they need you. This will allow you to keep the upper hand. It's all a mind game.

You can't look at life in terms of 123's and ABC's. Always have a master plan and train your mind to think deeply and manipulatively. If you don't, you will lose. Let's keep it real, we all play mind games. A woman tells you she loves you but she's never home and always claims to be with her girls, it's game. Then you ask her to go to the movies and she says she doesn't feel well. She's playing with your head. That's when you act like you're going by yourself. You then have a friend call her and tell her she won tickets to go to a Maxwell concert because you know she loves Maxwell. When she goes to pick up the tickets, walk up behind her and tell her she's full of shit.

If someone plays mind games with you, do the same to them. Set traps for them. Make them respect your mind. Ladies, if you want to catch your dude in a lie, use psychology to do it. If he says he's going to Wal-Mart and you don't believe him, say to him, "Baby, I heard there was a bad accident on the freeway on the way to Wal-Mart." If he's lying, he's going to hesitate. If he's telling the truth, he's going to tell you there was no backed up traffic. I love to work my mind and I can assure you that if you master this art and exercise your brain, you will be a master human chess player.

THE BREAKDOWN

When I was in the game, I had to use my mind to control everyone around me. I was a sharp dresser which was a tactic I used to let everyone know that I was on top of my game. Dressing nice is a must in the street game because no woman wants to kick it with a nigga that looks broke. I had to mentally break down the girls that rode with me who would try the same tactics they used on their tricks at home with me. I needed to set an example and a precedence in my household that I wasn't about to put up with any bullshit. Niggas in the game would lay low to knock me for a bitch and I had to stay on my P's and Q's in order to maintain the upper hand.

In all aspects and facets of life, use your mind to outwit your opponent. Use any tactic available that will confuse or outfox your enemy. The right colors, questions, and scenarios presented to your opponent may throw them off and weaken their game. You must always prepare yourself psychologically for the fight and win in your mind before you enter into battle. Do research on your enemy. Find out what makes them angry. Tap into their weaknesses and use them to your advantage. When you are mentally ready, it will be near impossible for you to be defeated.

The Art of Persuasion

When I was five, my big brother put me on his sales team. This consisted of going to the local stores and stealing sunglasses, cologne and whatever we could sell. After we would do this dumb shit, he would sit me down and say, "'Lil bro, the key to selling is never letting them get a word in. Just keep talking to them and make them buy it. Tell them that you're hungry, it's for the church or school supplies. It don't make a difference just as long as they buy."

My brother was a child himself but his persuasive skills were way up there. I watched him for weeks until I had the game and before you knew it, I could sell water to a well. Most people don't know it but they use persuasion every day. For example, when a woman wants sex from her husband, she puts on something sexy and calls him sweet names, etc. When a man wants sex from his significant other, he goes out and buys her perfumes, purses and he too becomes extra friendly. This is the art of persuasion. When we want something, we come up with clever shit all the time.

I remember many years ago when I was in the street life if I wanted a female to be on my team, I would persuade her that she would have a better life with me and we were going to the top. To do this, I would have to employ some slick human chess moves. For example, I would say, "Hey, baby I been thinking about something and I really think that you and I are the one." This is a common saying amongst persuaders in this field, however it works because women like to be told they are the one even though it's bullshit. But it's what you do as a human chess player and a professional persuader. Then I would say, "If you can only give me your all and follow my instructions, I can take you to the promised land."

She would ask me, "What's in it for me?"

This is when you close the deal and persuade her to believe

114

that it's worth it. "Baby, you're going to get to be with me, drive the best cars, wear mink coats and live in the big house with Ken." The cars and minks don't mean shit to her what she really wants is Ken. A good persuader understands that it makes no difference what you say in the beginning or the middle as long as you make your target understand your main point in the end. I understood that I was a nice looking guy and women liked me, but for me to like them, they had to do something for me so my conversation was always filled with the things I wanted while at the same time building my prospect up to believe that I wanted them.

Some of the best human chess players and persuaders are insurance and car salesmen and women. Every time I go to buy a car for a budget of $40K, the car salesman convinces me to buy the car with the most features, the one the girls are going to love and the one with more room for my family. You have to give it to them. They are some slick operators. Insurance is a good thing to have, but they don't just want you to have burial insurance so you can have a nice casket and a decent funeral. By the time you leave that insurance office they're going to persuade you that if you don't buy life insurance, your kids are going to be out on the streets and your wife is going to be forced to find another husband to take care of your children because you left her no money. The last thing a jealous husband wants to think about is another man sexing his wife when he's dead and gone.

While I was in prison, I read many books on how to persuade and how to sell. Books like *The Greatest Salesman in the World* by Og Mandino, *Outwitting the Devil: The Secret to Freedom and Success* by Napoleon Hill and *How to Win Friends and Influence People* by Dale Carnegie. These books sharpened my game and gave me the confidence and skills I need to help me become more adept at human chess and the art of persuasion. If I put my mind to it, I can talk a fish out if water. I'm no longer that little boy who was stealing with his big brother and telling all the other kids lies to sell our stolen goods. I am now a master at human chess and a hell of a persuader.

THE BREAKDOWN

There are some people out there that are so good at the art of persuasion that they are called charmers. And they can even charm a snake. A lot of squares call them conmen and swindlers but no matter what we do in life, we are going to persuade or be persuaded. I strongly advise you to learn as much as you can about this art even if it's only to keep the cheater off of you.

As a human chess player, you're going to need to persuade your opponents to go left when you're going right. You need to be persuasive to get that management job you want so badly. When the United States Senate and Congress refuse to work with Barack Obama, he had to persuade the auto industry, the banks and businessmen and women to work with him to help build the economy back and get the unemployment rate down. In the streets, you don't just become that dude you have to persuade people to know that you're the best.

Whenever I left my house, I had the thousand dollar shoes on, the $2500 suit and drove the high end luxury whips. My purpose was to let anyone out there know that was paying attention that I'm not playing. It offends most but it convinced all that I was one of the best to ever do it and get away with it. I was selling me and persuading them to believe I was who I said I was. Be the best you can be at whatever you do but make sure you master the art of persuasion. There is nothing you will do as a human that will not require human chess and persuasion. These two go hand in hand.

Lastly, had I not mastered the art of persuasion, I would have never been able to negotiate with multi-million dollar corporations like HBO and Simon & Schuster and receive six figures. Being persuasive works, so don't leave home without this tool in your toolbox.

The Art of Disappearing

In order to build a brand and a name, you have to market yourself. Use any and every opportunity to promote your name. This is important because no one pays attention to a nobody. They only respond to the famous and well-respected. But once you reach this status, you have to know when to disappear. Why? Because people become complacent and start looking at you as their equal. They start asking you questions like, "Why are you not doing the TV thing? Are you ok? Do you need help?" These questions are only meant to insult you and tell you in a nice way, "We don't want your famous ass around us." You have to disappear for a year, get missing so you won't lose your value. Once you're off the scene for a minute, they will start asking, "Where is Ken?" and this is where you want them.

When I was in my former game, I would go to a city with my best bitches, shine on them for about a month and as soon as they got comfortable with me and think I was on their level, I would disappear from the group. When this happened and they didn't see me for a week or so, I would get calls from everywhere asking, "Where are you man? Dude, everybody's been looking for you. Are you ok? When are you coming back?" This is how it goes when you're playing human chess. Give them just enough of your time to like you and then remove yourself from them. I can assure you that they will all be asking about you and saying, "That's my dude. I miss him."

People will never know that you are using the art of disappearing to make yourself more liked and missed. Think about when you go to a family reunion and see relatives that you haven't seen in a long time. Every time I go to my family reunion, I see people I haven't seen in years and I'm genuinely happy to see them. Then I see the family that I see all the time and I pay them no attention. The art of disappearing helps you to stay above your competition and to always stay fresh even if it means you have to stay gone for long periods of time. In the end, you will protect your brand and keep your name good.

One person that has mastered this human chess move is the famous producer and rapper Dr. Dre. Dre puts out an album about every ten years and every time he releases one, he sells millions of records and this is because he doesn't saturate us with music like most artists do. Dre give us his best beats, features and plenty of marketing. And just when his fans are screaming for more, he disappears.

Dr. Dre's last album was in 2000. Then he was quiet for years other than making beats and working with his artists. Out of nowhere he shocked the world by coming out with *Beats by Dre*, a set of headphones that cost $300. His fans and the general public rushed to get a set. Because Dr. Dre had been off the scene so long, everyone bought his headphones and he became Hip Hop's first billionaire.

When people ask me, "Ken, why haven't you written a book, done a DVD or worked with celebrities in seven years?" I have done a lot, appeared on numerous records and worked with everyone in the industry. It was time to disappear and reinvent myself and my career and find a new way to reappear. As a master human chess player, I never missed the people and fame because I knew I was going to come with new ideas and plans. I wasn't the most respected in the streets because I was rich or had the best skills. I was respected because I knew when to get out of the way and be missed.

THE BREAKDOWN

You can attend Harvard, Yale, Princeton, Howard, Alverno or any prestigious college and they won't teach you how to win in this game of life. That's why it's very important that you master these arts and principles in order to become a master human chess player. The mistake most leaders and entertainers make is not knowing when to disappear and be missed. This is why you have so many one hit wonders in the music business. One day they have a hit record, video on BET, MTV and touring all over the world. A year later, they can't give their music away.

Look at artists like Prince, Beyoncé, Jay-Z and Usher. They make a hit then they go away for awhile to let us miss them. This leaves their fans wanting more. This is a great tactic and if you use it correctly, you will never play out. I don't get stuck on what I have done in my past, I just move on to the next project in corporate America. They call this innovation or the S curve. Be popular, have a big brand but when they become too familiar with you, disappear and reinvent yourself. This is the practice of all masters of human chess.

The Art of Charming

There is no way that you will get far in life without a pleasing personality. You have to be fun to be around and people have to look to you as the person that can calm things down. When I first got in the game, I was always mad and didn't care who liked it. It was this attitude that landed me in prison. While I was in prison, one of the books I read was *Success Through a Positive Mental Attitude* by Napoleon Hill. This book put me on the right track and I used it to help me deal with all the killers and gangsters in prison. I learned that a smile will disarm even the coldest person and a handshake was a sign of a peace agreement. Humor makes people laugh and as long as they have a smile on their face, they can't be on some bullshit.

I read books on body language and mastered how people talk with their body. Once I was released, I used these tools to outsmart my competition and win over a lot of people. You can say what you want about me, but no one can deny that I was the most loved non-rapper in Hip Hop. Everyone wanted to work with me and have me be a part of their projects. This was only because I was a master at the art of charming.

When you see people get arrested, the first thing they do is sick that mean ass cop on you. He calls you names and accuses you of doing whatever the charge is and promises you that you're going to spend the rest of your life in jail. Then out of nowhere this clean-cut, very respectable detective comes in talking nice and offering you coffee. He tells you he's here to help you if you help him. This is the charm game he's running and I've heard that 60% of criminals confess to this charming officer.

I travel all over the United States and every business that I visit that is owned by a major corporation has employees that greet you with a charming smile. No one wants to do business with a saleswoman that mean mugs them or with a banker that gives them the middle finger when they enter the bank. Learn to smile, have a good handshake and spit good conversation and you will master the art of charm like a good human chess player should.

THE BREAKDOWN

Being charming is not an easy task and could take years to perfect. This is why I say study the master and you will advance sooner than you think. President Bill Clinton is a master at charming anyone and he knows how to win people over in a heartbeat. Just study how he smiles and always has something insightful to say. Democrats worked with him but a lot of Republicans did, too. Rev. Dr. Martin Luther King, Jr. was a great thinker, but it was his charm that helped him win over the millions of people that he did. I used to love to charm women because I knew all of them were looking for Prince Charming. Let's keep it real, you catch more bees with honey than you do with vinegar. So step your charm game up and read books like the *The Power of Charm: How to Win Anyone Over in Any Situation* by Brian Tracy and *Get Anyone to Do Anything* by David J. Lieberman, PhD.

The Art of Getting Attention

Let's face it. You can master everything about human chess, but if no one knows you or sees you, it's all in vain. When I present a new product, my job is to make sure everyone knows about it and sees it. For example, for this book, I will personally drive across the United States visiting every radio station and hand deliver my book to their program directors and DJs. I do this to show respect and appreciation, plus it's good for them to have a surprise famous guest.

I plan to print thousands of books and sell them out of the trunk. People love when they can meet the famous person behind the body of work. Plus the best promotion is by word of mouth. Who is not going to tell a friend they bought a book from Pimpin' Ken personally at the mall, barber shop or the club? I'm doing this to get attention and more sales, it's an art. I will also have all of my celebrity friends do one minute YouTube videos telling people to buy *The Art of Human Chess: A Study Guide to Winning*. I will buy ads in magazines, appear on talk shows and promote on social media.

Wise business people know publicity sells products, and no company can make it without getting the word out to the people that there is a new product on the market. Getting attention for most people started when they were very young, being the class clown, a pretty girl or nice dresser. In the game, you had to be an attention-getter because it's a flashy lifestyle and the women love the flash. They see the rappers and singers with all that shiny stuff and want you to look like them. I didn't have the rappers' money when I was in the streets, but I damn sure had their look. In my old life, we called this a campaign and if you didn't have a good one, you didn't last long. Look at some of the old movies from back then. Dudes had the big hats, wore funny colors, stacked shoes that were about three inches high, and cars with bears and stars carved on the back windows. All this was for attention. Attention is a good thing in the art of human chess if it gets you paid.

THE BREAKDOWN

When you look at those old *Super Fly*, *Willie Dynamite* and *The Mack* movies, you can't help but say, "Damn, they were some clowns." But if you think about it, that was how they ate, by being flamboyant. Michael Jackson was the best-selling artist of all time, but if he didn't look different, dance wild and wear that sequin glove, would he have gotten our attention? If Donald Trump didn't have that funny haircut, would he be famous? Would you know Don King without his crown of a hairstyle? Elvis Presley is still banking off of his image, and he's been dead for years. All these people made millions being attention-seekers. Get lots of attention and you will make money and be well-known.

The Art of Seduction

Often times we think of seduction as a way to get a man or a woman. But in reality it's used in business, politics, religion and acquiring love. Being a former player, I had to use the art of seduction every day. I would meet a woman that I wanted on my team and I would instantly say sweet things to her like, "Damn baby, you so fine if beauty was a crime, you would be charged with a felony. Damn girl, have you ever thought about being a nurse? Because you will make a sick P pockets well." If you're good at talking shit, this is a good way to seduce someone.

People like colorful words, and since man can remember, we have used communication to get what we want from people. When a pretty girl tells a nerdy-type of guy that she loves him, it drives him crazy. At that point she can get him to do whatever she wants, even if it causes him to lose his job or other positive things that he has going on in his life. How many times have we read the headlines in a newspaper, "Man/woman kills mate and runs away with mystery person." This is because this person was heavily seduced by a younger person or someone that has penetrated their mind, usually through sex. This is the most common form of seduction.

If you ever study politics, you will see that most politicians use a more subtle form of the art of seduction. A politician can be the most devious person in the world. His charisma, smile and words of hope blind the public and make everyone think that he is the squarest person on the planet. You go out to vote for him because he has charmed you and won you over. President John F. Kennedy was a great American President, however he was rumored to have had an affair with Marilyn Monroe. President Bill Clinton was the most believable President of our time, but he was said to have an affair with Monica Lewinsky. Barack Obama was loved by the Black community when he was running for office, but now they feel he has not done enough to help them. What people need to understand is that these Presidents have mastered the art of seduction and will say what they need to say in order to win your vote. They are human chess players and they're going to plan, plot and strategize to win at the game of politics.

Seduction is a chess game and to the victor go the spoils. Do you remember the television show *How to Catch a Predator*? This show was deception and seduction at its finest. Basically, the producers of the show would hire a young pretty girl that would chat with these freaks, AKA predators, online. They would tell the predator that they were sixteen and act like they like older men. After the young actress would seduce the predator into thinking they wanted to have sex, the pedophile would travel to the set-up spot, meet the girl and out of the blue, a reporter would come and expose the predator. They always try to run only to find the police waiting for their ass. What was the motive? Sex with a minor and that shit ain't cool.

Men have been lured by sex from the beginning of time. Great human chess players never let sex be the reason for their moves, but if necessary will use sex to trap or outfox their opponent. When I was in Vegas, I watched the vice police use seduction to trap the pimps. An undercover posing as a young blond prostitute would get the pimp's number and call him saying, "Hey baby, my name is

Candy and I heard you were the top pimp and I want to choose a pimp." Believe it or not, ninety percent of the pimps fall for this false seduction.

In the book *The Art of Seduction*, Robert Greene says that before Cleopatra and the other great seductresses of our time, men would use force in business, politics and all walks of life. During this time, the women had to find ways to gain control. They knew they couldn't win through physical force so they developed the art of seduction. They began to use sex, smiles and sweet conversation to seduce the men of this time. This method was so effective that the men began to use it as well. Once they started using this, violence slowed down and the human chess players began to pride themselves as thinkers, persuaders and manipulators. Learn to seduce and you will win in most situations. One thing about a good chess player is that he or she will do whatever they have to do in order to win.

THE BREAKDOWN

Seducing one another has been around since the beginning of time. I'm not sure what made Adam eat that apple, but it may have had something to do with Eve's fine ass. Seduction is seen in all aspects of selling. When you look at a commercial for liquor, there are beautiful people enjoying themselves, dancing and playing the piano. The commercial makes you want to go out and buy the liquor so you can feel the way they feel. Seduction is an essential part of persuasion. If you can seduce someone, it is more likely that they will side with you and do what you want them to do.

Cleopatra used seduction as a tool to take over an empire. Had she not been smart enough to know that her beauty and cunning tactics would ultimately lead her back into power, history as we know it would be completely different. The art of seduction must be used in human chess. Mastering this art will take you far in this game.

The Art of War

Make no mistake about it. You are going to have enemies until the day you die. When I was in first grade, there was this 'lil punk named Derrick who would hate on me to our teacher. He would tell on me for everything I did. We would be on the playground and he would bump into me for no reason at all. I was only six years old but I hated that 'lil motha fucka. One day after school, I asked my dad, "Why is Derrick always picking on me?"

Pops got right to the point, "Kick his ass. He'll stop messing with you."

I saw him in the lunchroom and I slapped the shit out of him. He jumped up and we fought for a few minutes and he ended up biting me on my neck. From that day on, wherever I saw him, we would fight. Dude was considered an enemy then and is one now. Biting me was a declaration of war. This was kid shit, but war is a serious thing and as a human chess player, you must know the rules of engagement. If someone claims to be a friend and then goes behind your back, they are at that point considered an enemy. You can pretend you don't know and let them think y'all are still cool or you can cut them off right away. As a human chess player, it's important to let your opponent know that you're not interested in false friendship.

When at war with someone, you have to know everything about your enemy including his strengths, weaknesses and his position. Knowing this will give you the advantage. Always keep spies on your team, people that befriend your enemy and come back and report to you their position and plans. Chess is about planning, plotting and strategies. The man or woman that is most skilled in these areas will win most of their battles. Wars have been going on since man has been on this planet. To be a boss and not know the rules of engagement is a grave mistake on your part. People love to interact with one another and as long as we continue to do this, we are going to create enemies and haters that we must defend ourselves against.

For example, look at all the reality shows out there. They all start off with the cast being cool but by the end of the series, they are all at war. Even in business you see merger takeovers. Large companies buy out the smaller ones, eliminating their competition. The United States will view any country as an enemy that doesn't share our values and will send the CIA, FBI and any other agency to see what's up with them. The US will give leaflets to the people to try and get them to overthrow their government. War is serious and the man that plays for keeps wins.

When I was younger, we had what was called "The War on Drugs." Those drug dealers back then would shoot up the next drug dealer's spot, kidnap family members and even go to the police on one another just to gain control of a certain area. It was sad but it was war and in war someone has to lose. The person who employs the smarter tactics will be the victor. I urge that you never fall asleep, and when you find yourself at war, use whatever means you have at your disposal to win. This is a serious art that must be mastered in order to keep you from losing your position, business or even your life.

The Republicans hate Barak Obama and when he first came in office they declared war against him. Just look at some of the things they did. They never voted on one of his policies unless he changed it to a bill that was damn near a Republican bill. They never met with him unless they had no other option. They called him all kinds of names, threatened to impeach him and once interrupted him during a State of the Union Address. Obama never took it personally. He understood that all is fair in war and that you couldn't put anything past your enemies. Democrats felt disrespected because of the way the Republicans treated the President.

Drastic times called for drastic measures and most of the moves that the President took were to counter his enemies. He eventually got gas prices down to $1.99 in some areas, reduced the unemployment rate, ended two wars and killed the man who claimed responsibility for September 11th. It was war. President Obama did what he had to do and the Republicans did what they had to do.

Being at war with Derrick prepared me for the wars I would encounter later in my career. From the time I did the movie with HBO until now, I have had motha fuckas trying to plot on me. All these guys out here want to be the next Pimpin' Ken and I don't blame them. But the cross-out shit that I've been through was totally unnecessary.

I now use my mind to crush my opponent. When they talk about me, I remain quiet and refuse to respond because I don't want to give them any airplay. If they are a friend and they decide to cross me, I just change my number and cut them off. When they congregate and try teaming up on me, I disappear and don't do anything. This makes them look like some high-powered haters. I love to go to war because my only revenge is success. Outthink your haters and enemies and never let them catch you slipping. Use the secrets in this book to win and stay on top of your game.

THE BREAKDOWN

From the time we are children, we are at war in some sort. Whether it is on the playground as schoolmates or in the White House as the President of the United States, war is simply when you are fighting against an enemy. You must first prepare yourself to engage in a fight. When Floyd Mayweather agrees to a fight, he sets a date and begins to train vigorously every day until the day of the fight. He watches the fights of his opponent and studies his style and mannerisms. He does this so that he is prepared to fight his enemy on the scheduled date.

In life, we have mini-wars every day. The key is to be prepared for everything. I always say that no matter what, I am ready for tomorrow. I'm not a psychic and I have no idea what tomorrow is going to bring, but God willing that I wake up tomorrow, I'd better be ready. The art of war mostly entails being prepared. Without preparation in war, you will surely lose.

Chess Notes

Chapter Sixteen
The Methods and Tactics I Used To Get in Good Grace With the Celebrities

"Those who know that life comes with ebbs and flows, and that you have to ride those waves, will be successful."

~Excerpt from:
Pimpin' Ken and Karen Hunter
Pimpology/The 48 Laws of the Game
Published by Simon & Schuster~

*"Not everything that can be counted counts,
and not everything that counts can be counted."*
~Albert Einstein~

This book gives you a lot of tricks to use to get ahead in life, but sometimes just being a real dude and a stand up gentleman can take you far. I have had the privilege to work with some of the richest and most powerful people in the music business. It was because of these relationships that my brand became so big and I remain relevant today. Is this human chess? Yes it is and I will show you how being real can get you friendships money can't buy.

P. Diddy

P. Diddy is a smart businessman and I knew it would not be wise to just walk up to him and ask him to work with me. So I made it my business to find someone that knew him and worked with him. To me as a human chess player, this is a very intelligent tactic because it makes a person comfortable to meet someone new that was introduced by a person that they trust. The person I picked was Loom, the Bad Boy rapper from New York. I admit I didn't know Loom that well, but we had a mutual friend who was an accountant that knew him and she would tell me shit like, "Loom is the next nigga," and that he wrote for Diddy.

One day I called her and said, "Can you hook me up with Loom?" She did, and Loom and I became cool. Loom heard about my ability to do intros and outros so he asked me to be on his album. I did the album and I knew that this was my chance to meet one of my favorite businessmen. Diddy liked what I did for the album and he had his people call me. They asked me what I wanted and I said, "I want to meet Puff and I want Loom to do a free show for me in Milwaukee at the Park Bar." By this time, Loom was famous and all over BET, MTV and the radio. They agreed and Loom performed a successful show. P. Diddy flew me first class to Atlanta and got me a suite in a 5-Star hotel and let only me into his personal VIP booth. He also appeared in my DVD *The Ghetto Streets to the Executive Suites* out of love.

Let's keep it real. Anyone can't just walk up to a man that's worth $500M and befriend him. But because I used my human chess skills, I was able to meet the King and work with him. Human chess really works. You just have to use your brain.

50 Cent

I met 50 Cent through Dave, my Limo driver from Cut Above Limo. Dave would let me know when someone important was in town. So one day, Dave called me and said, "Hey man! I'm chilling with 50 Cent." This was at the beginning of 50's career and he was the hottest rapper in the world. I had one thing to my advantage: 50 Cent recorded a song called *Problem Child* and he mentioned my name in that song. I told Dave, "Man, you got to let me know where 'lil buddy is going to be. I need to work with him."

Dave pulled up at the Embassy Suites with 50 and I waited for him to get out the car and said, "Hey 50. Pimpin' Ken." Dude was a fan and we did a commercial for my movie and he got down with an interview for it. Now what y'all need to understand is that 50 was charging hundreds of thousands just to talk to him, but being the good dude he is, he did it for me for free. There is no way I could have paid for all that love and I would have never gotten that love had I not been wise enough to use Dave as a human pawn to let me know that 50 was in town. I got 50's manager Sha Money's number and he called me every time they were doing something.

One day he called me and said, "Ken, come to Jackson Mississippi. We have ten shows to do for Master P."

I knew I wasn't going to go all the way to Mississippi for nothing. Like I said, 50 was the biggest artist in the world, so I went to the show and told the DJ that I'm opening the show for 50 Cent. The DJ gave me the mic and I said, "Ladies and gentlemen! I have one of the biggest stars in the world coming to the stage! None other than 50 Cent." 50 Cent came out to the stage and said, "Y'all give it up for my dog, Pimpin' Ken."

As a human chess player, you have to strategize and plan and make sure your next move is your best move. I attended four more shows and I got cool with them. Next, they called me to do the P.I.M.P. video. They paid me and 50 told the director to let me say my name in the video. At the time of writing this book, that video has had over sixty million views on YouTube and was seen over eighty million times on networks like MTV and BET. Now that's human chess for that ass. Can you imagine how much it would have cost me for all that advertising had 50 not showed me love? I also hosted a mixtape for 50 and all this came from me using my man Dave as a human chess pawn. You have to play chess to get on top.

'Lil Jon

One day, the rapper Too $hort and I were chilling at his house and I said, "Shit, man. You got to plug me with that dude 'Lil Jon."

He said, "Nigga, that's crazy because I'm about to go do a video with him right now."

We got in our cars and went to the video shoot. I met 'Lil Jon and we exchange numbers. One day he called me and we went to a club together to kick it. We were in the club and not one person went up to 'Lil Jon. I asked him, "How can you have the number one record in the south and no one knows you are the artist?"

He smiled and said, "They will know."

I'm a good human chess player and you don't always have to run game to be great. Being real can also help you become a master at human chess. So I kept it real with 'Lil Jon and said, "Pimp, if you buy a pimp cup and put your name on it, your fan base will jump off big time." I sold him a cup and he became larger than life. He gave Paris Hilton and many other stars a cup and the pimp cup became famous.

Everywhere 'Lil Jon went they would interview him about his cup. One day he did an interview in *XXL Magazine* and they asked him where he got his cup from and he replied, "Pimpin' Ken." Being a good human chess player sometimes allows you to bless others and the blessing can come back on you and that's some real shit. Since then, I appeared on two of 'Lil Jon's albums and about four of his music videos.

It's chess, baby. The videos were once again viewed by millions on MTV, BET and YouTube. The albums sold over 8M records. That was love and it gave me advertising I couldn't have paid for. I knew that cup would help 'Lil Jon grow as well as remember me.

Jermaine Dupri

Jermaine Dupri was the Mayor of the Atlanta music scene back in the early 90s and parts of 2000. If he didn't fuck with you, ATL didn't fuck with you. I needed him to fuck we me so I could put my moves down in the A. So I came up with this practical strategy. I would go to all the clubs he hung out at and when he was in the house, I would buy the bar for fifteen minutes. I figured that they could only serve about $200-300 worth of liqueur in fifteen minutes. The DJ would be on the mic for the next fifteen minutes saying, "Drinks are on Pimpin' Ken!" I would then walk through the crowd shaking everyone's hands so Jermaine Dupri would see the people showing me love.

I did this until one day Jermaine came up to me and said "What's up, Pimpin'?" In my mind I was saying, "I'm talking to the Mayor of the ATL music game." I was sharp enough to know that he did his research on me. I was playing chess letting Jermaine see I'm a money nigga and that I had love in his town. He said, "Man, I need you on my album." Once that record dropped, all of ATL fucked with Pimpin' Ken and at the time, ATL was running the game. Here I was, Ken Ivy from the small city of Milwaukee getting major love in the A. If you are a master human chess player, there is nothing you can't do.

Pimp C

All I can say about Pimp C is that he is one of the most stand up men and friends I have ever had (Rest in peace, my brother). I met him at Sharp Towns mall in Houston, Texas and he saw me first. He yelled, "Is that Pimpin' Ken?" What I didn't know then but later found out was that Pimp C was a big fan of the documentary *Pimps Up, Ho's Down*. I replied, "Yeah. Is that Pimp C from UGK?" It turned out we were fans of each other. At that point we became partners in human chess, like partners in crime and started working together playing chess as a team.

One day I was spending the night over his Mom's crib and he said, "Ken, man, I want you to tell these MFs you're a producer. These niggas ain't making their own beats anyway."

I replied, "Young nigga, I like that. You full of game."

From then on, we agreed to work together. The first thing we did was get on each other's albums. We would go out everywhere together so people could see we were a team. Our plan was to put out a pimp compilation. Unfortunately, Pimp went to jail for four years. But we never stopped plotting and strategizing. I would visit and write him. Once he came home, we did a documentary called

The Best of Both Worlds. We were in there clowning showing money, jewelry our big cribs and our love for each other. This was to let people know that we were one and that we were about to take over.

The DVD sold big time and it positioned Rick, Pimp's manager, for an opportunity to get us a five movie deal for $3M. The first movies were going to be about my life and Pimp was going to play me. Right after the deal was made, he went on YouTube and said, "Nobody can play Ken like me." Now that we had something to work with, we began to put more chess moves down. Pimp was a smart businessman and he would always say, "Ken, your name is Pimpin' Ken the pimp and I'm Pimp C the rapper. We're going to fuck these niggas up with this collab." He put me on his next four albums including the last UGK album which sold over a million copies. He put me in all his videos and mentioned me on the radio all the time. It was all human chess getting people ready for the Pimp C and Pimpin' Ken brand. Then, out of nowhere tragedy struck. My friend died in Los Angeles. RIP to one of the best human chess players I ever worked with and one of the best friends that I have ever known.

THE BREAKDOWN

What I did in the music business has never been done. There is no record of a dude from a small town going into the music business that can't rap or sing and appearing on over twenty major albums with platinum artists and is featured in over thirty major music videos. This was the best marketing plan ever and if I would have had to pay for it, it would have cost me millions. All I had to do was keep it real with these cats. I'm a human chess player and a good dude. You could get lucky and work with maybe one celebrity, but I worked with multiple people on different levels. I did *The Way We Ball* video with 'Lil Flip, *Hot In Herre* with Nelly, I did two albums with Pastor Troy, three videos with Juvenile from Cash Money Records, *So Fresh, So Clean* with Outkast and two albums with west coast rapper Mack 10. I was also featured in movies with Katt Williams and Clifton Powell, who played Pinky on *Friday*.

Either I'm lucky or I'm a real dude and everyone recognizes it.

Chess Notes

Chapter Seventeen
People That I Personally Know As Human Chess Players

"A strong captain communicates your vision, enforces it, and inspires your team to really want to win."

~Excerpt from:
Pimpin' Ken and Karen Hunter
Pimpology/The 48 Laws of the Game
Published by Simon & Schuster~

"I have surrounded myself with very smart people."
~Dolly Parton~

Over the years I have encountered many people and one thing that I found out is that people are very peculiar with many shades and many colors. And the interesting thing is that the people that I personally know in this chapter are very charismatic and skillful in the art of human chess. Therefore, I have selected to show the reader that the art of human chess is not exclusive to people in entertainment, politics or business. Everyday people can be just as shroud and creative as anyone else. It is my hope that by you reading these brief stories of my personal associates it would give you the confidence and desire to become a master human chess player.

Baby
The Female Serpent

One of the most ruthless, cold-hearted female human chess players that I know is a veteran entertainer by the name of Baby. She had no teacher, mentor or life-coach. She was born to be a female beast. She was a dancer and the club was her chessboard. From the time she walked in until the time she left, her game clock was on. Before she would even step in the door, she would lay low in the parking lot to scan the perimeter to see what caliber of customers were patronizing the joint. Once she had a read, she would enter the building looking very square. Her reason was she didn't want the customers to know that she was the girl that would eventually take them on a long cash trip.

Once inside, she would begin her payola. She gave the DJ $50 so he wouldn't call her on stage. Baby understood that you can't make big money on stage unless there was a baller in the house trying to show everyone that he had paper. She knew that the young girls liked to get rained on so she let them have that. In most cases, the average person making it rain may throw $300-500. To the onlooker that looks like a lot of money. Not to Baby. She doesn't want anything to do with that stage.

She is a human chess player and her strategy is to plot on that one guy with the unlimited credit card and isolate him from all the competition. In that type of environment, you have to isolate your customer because there are lots of pretty girls with no game and they would do a lot more for less. She would grab the customer by the hand and say, "Honey, come with me. I would like to show you something." She would take them into the VIP area and say, "This is the champagne room. It's $500 for the half hour and a thousand for the hour. The good thing about it is I'm going to be your sexy pussycat until you have had all the fun you can pay for." Not all of the customers would go for this, but when they did, she would take over their minds until their credit cards were maxed out.

Baby would call a waitress into her champagne room and tell her, "This is my friend. He and I are going to play this game called drink me under the table." Baby was very tactful so what she would do is pay the waitress off by having her bring her water in a shot glass to make the guy think it was vodka while she brings him pure vodka. After a few drinks, he is ready to marry Baby. This is when Baby would talk very dominant to him saying things like, "Who is your fucking Mami? Who's the fucking boss? Who do you fucking love?" At this point, he's so drunk he believes everything she says.

When Baby's time would end in the champagne room, she was not finished. It's time for another hour and Baby would ask him for his credit card. In order to pay for a VIP, the customer has to fingerprint and sign his name on the credit card slip. This makes it legit and before she would give it to the manager, she would ask the happy drunk customer for a tip. They would always say yes. She would ask them to write in a tip for a stack and then turn in the slips to her manager. Just like that, she would make $2K. Now she has another hour to run her game.

Baby would order food, use the restroom and do anything to pass up the time. When the waitress says, "The room is up in fifteen minutes," Baby, who was always planning her next move, would leave the room and go get another girl and ask her customer, "Honey, don't you want to see me and my girl kiss on each other?" This is just to get him aroused and ready for round three. It worked all the time if the guy had the money in the account. And if he didn't, Baby had another trick. She would take them to a nearby casino and show them how to withdraw credit from the casino. Any casino in America will give you whatever is in your bank account for fifteen percent of the transaction.

Once the transaction was complete at the casino, she would take them back to the club where there's cameras and club security. Baby was a master at the game and she was the baddest chick at every club. The girls hated her because she was about her money. She hated them too, so whenever she saw a girl sitting with a rich-looking customer, she would go give the DJ $50 to call the lame chick up on stage and then go steal her customer. Sometimes if it was slow, she would have all the pretty girls sit with her and her customer to buy them drinks so they would get drunk and couldn't think. She used everyone as pawns and ruled wherever she worked. She is a boss bitch and everyone that has ever met her will say the same thing. Her skills at human chess are unbelievable.

I once heard that a guy met her and was so impressed with her that he offered her an upper-level management position at his company. She tested him and said, "If you're serious, send me nine stacks." He did and she told him, "You can't afford me." Baby kept the money and said, "I owe you a VIP next time I see you."

Baby was heartless and like a bee, would sting anyone that got in her way. She's the type of woman that doesn't even want a man. She's so cold-hearted, she once drove a weak ass nigga she was fucking with so crazy, he ended up in a mental hospital in Atlanta. A strong woman needs an even stronger man or she will eat you alive.

Like Jay-Z, Baby can make it anywhere. She has a master's degree and is very beautiful, educated, manipulative, deceptive and she thinks like a very powerful man that had to step on many toes to get to the top. I know a lot of slick women but none of them come close to Baby. Baby, you are the best female human chess player I have ever encountered.

Marvin Ivy
My 'Lil Bro

I can remember my Pops sitting us down to give us some game and my little brother Marvin was so young, he wasn't even paying attention. He would be playing with toys and doing him. I on the other hand would be glued to my father's every word. I became this street dude and was in jail by the age of nine for pulling a fire alarm. Marvin had other plans. By the time he was nine, he was the number one paper boy in the state and a few years later he was on a plane to England paid for by *Milwaukee Journal*. He was so slick that he had the other kids on the block working for him and that's why his route was the biggest one. He was showing human chess skills at a very young age.

Marvin was so good with people and outfoxing his competitors that by the time he reached high school, the *Milwaukee Journal* wanted him to become a manager. Marvin was a planner and strategist. So he left the *Milwaukee Journal* and went to Chicago to work for my uncle Wade Ivy who had a carpet business. While he was doing all this, I was in prison. By the time he came back to Milwaukee, I had been released from jail and was hoping he would join me in my foolishness. I was able to get him to think about it for a minute. Then out of nowhere, he said, "Big bro, you're my idol but I can't be doing crimes. I'm about to start my own business."

I said, "Man, you're going to need money to get a business started."

He said, "Not really. My plan is to put out three thousand

144

flyers and see who calls me back." He did that and about five hundred people called him back and just like that, my brother was in business. I have to admit that he is the smartest out of the five of us boys because he has never been to the joint while the rest of us have.

I knew my brother was a strategist, but his next move blew my mind. He called me and said, "Big brother, I'm giving my life to God." A year later, he bought a new Benz and a home. I didn't say it then, but as I think about now I have to say that him joining the church was a good chess move because not only did he do the carpet of his church members, he also did the carpet for most of the big churches in Milwaukee. He may not be in the streets, but he is just as clever as any street cat I know.

Those carpet days are over and he is now the CEO of his own magazine, *Anointed Pages*. Once again he came to me and said, "Bro, I got this idea to start a magazine."

I replied, "Come on, bro. You don't know anything about a magazine."

He said, "When I was nine, I started working for a magazine company and I was the youngest and top salesperson on their team. I've been in the church for fifteen years now. I've met worked with all the top preachers. I am a minister now and I know God's word and how to put it out there."

I interrupted him and asked, "How are you going to get the money to get started?"

He replied, "I'm on it. I have a deal with Bentley and they already paid me for the inside cover and back of the magazine. I also have many more advertisers who are already onboard. My ads are sold out. My first interview is with the biggest preacher in Milwaukee and I have secretly gotten interviews from other top preachers in the city."

I stopped him and asked, "So this is a local magazine?"

He looked at me crazy and replied, "No way! We already have the biggest writer in the business on our team. We have Miles Monroe as one of our chief writers. I have interviews coming up with Bishop Gilbert Patterson (RIP, the leader of the Church of God in Christ), Paula White, Paul Morton and TD Jakes."

I was impressed with his explanation of how he was going to

execute his magazine. I like the fact that he had planned many steps ahead. The magazine was released and he had a very good marketing plan. He took the magazine to all the churches and left samples in their libraries. He placed samples in office buildings, barber and beauty shops everywhere. He ordered a press pass and traveled all over the US, interviewing top gospel singers and leaders. My brother is a hell of a chess player and I'm just waiting to see what he will do next. In this story as well as the other examples in this book, is a message for the reader. You don't need money but you most maneuver, plan, plot, strategize and exercise extreme patience. These are the tools that are used in human chess. Master them.

Father John Devine, PKA JD
The Don of the East Side

I met John Devine way back in the day when we were both in the seventh grade and full of game. I was the quiet type back then and didn't really kick it with people like that. The reason is because I was raised by some boss players. My father and uncle were in the game. I knew about the street life from the time I could talk. The young dudes that were at my school were lames to me.

The only dude that I peeped that had some flavor was JD. I knew he was sharp because he would act like he was reading a schoolbook but on the inside he would be reading a magazine. I said to myself, "This is a slick dude right here. I like his style." But what puzzled me was how he was getting his schoolwork done.

One day we were in class and I saw this girl pass him a folder and he took it up to our teacher, Mr. Carter. I said to myself, "This cat is slick like me. I dig his game." The bell rang and I said to JD, "Say, player. I got these stolen watches. You know where I can drop them?" I came at him like that to see if he would give me a sucker response like, "Man, I ain't going to mess with no stolen goods."

146

Not JD. He replied, "Shit, man. Our teacher Mr. Carter will buy all that shit."

We sold the watches and have been cool with each other ever since. I didn't call it human chess back then but I peeped that JD was a master player the way he had the girls doing his schoolwork. We began to plot together and J would act like he didn't like me so he could get people to gamble with me. Because of my skills with the dice, we would win the money all the time.

JD came by my crib one day wearing some hundred dollar shoes and he said to me, "Ken, we ain't never going to get the respect from the older dudes if we don't dress for success." That was thirty-five years before this book was written but my man was plotting and planning at the young age of sixteen and the shit he was demonstrating are two of the tools that are used in the art of human chess.

Another thing I remember that let me know J was a strategist was when I went to pick him up so we could go stealing and he said, "Man, fuck that shit. Let's go snatch some jewelry and wear it around the pimps and players. Man, your daddy and Uncle Greasy are boss players. We can't be doing this petty shit anymore."

In my mind I was thinking this dude is calling me petty, but I could see that he had a point. The only problem I had was that shit was a felony and could get us sent up state as fast a cop could say, "Put your hands up." I must admit, JD's plan worked. We had big jewelry and we were accepted by the pimps and players all over town. The older players looked at us as up and coming bosses. He was a young thinker and we were coming up fast.

The streets started talking and we received word that some dudes were planning to rob us. Jay said, "'Lil bro, don't worry. I predicted this shit was going to happen." He pulled a .25 automatic out if his pocket and said, "Like I said. You must anticipate and never underestimate." There again, young JD was showing skills as a future human chess player. Well, someone did try to rob JD and he ended up in Waupun Penitentiary at the age of seventeen with twelve years for attempted murder. I went to prison a year later. We both landed prison sentences that we served in Kettle Moraine Correctional Institution where we read books and tightened up our game. I left Kettle Moraine and didn't see JD for almost eight years.

Before JD was released, I caught two felonies and was sent back to prison. J served his time and was released three years before me. I was hearing all kinds of shit like, "He's a gang member" and "He's selling this and selling that." We wrote but he kept it brief and would always say, "Ken, man. Just come home. I got you."

When I came home JD gave me a car, named me CEO of his clothing store and put money in my pocket. I said, "Damn, my nigga. You play chess with this game."

He replied, "You're right bro. This shit is chess. You have to plan and strategize on these suckers. Keep to yourself and only speak to your lawyer and family. They think I'm rich and sell drugs but I just treat everybody with respect and they come to my store to spend that hustle money with me. I own five houses on the block. I live in one and collect rent from the rest of them. Because of this, I can drive this Benz and that Jag."

JD has not been back to jail in thirty years. To me, it takes a master chess player to stay out of that hellish place. He's still riding Benz's and owns three houses on that same block. Once all the fame and attention started coming, JD said, "'Lil bro, these suckers are going to try and put us against each other. I'm going to fall back and let you take all the shine."

I respected this chess move. Because JD can talk just as slick as me and has some real boss game. His discussion was a good one because we never had any power struggles. Believe me, lots of people came to him saying shit like, "JD, you're better than Ken. You can do what he's doing better." JD would cuss them out and tell them, "Motha fucka, get out of my face. I'm not going to cross Kenny."

Now y'all know why I share my fame with him in my books and DVDs. He and I are chess players and we can see years down the road. It's been eighteen years since HBO came to Milwaukee and JD and I are still plotting up on that legit money, building our brands and making pro moves. I salute my brother and in my opinion, he is a master chess player.

There are a lot of negative things that people say about my dude, but I don't know too many guys his age that have accomplished the things he did. Just reflect on some of the things I wrote about him in my books. Thirty-seven years and we have never had a major argument. He is the perfect gentleman and if you upset him, he will outfox you and out-maneuver you in every way. He is a great human chess player and I know the best of my friend John Devine is yet to come.

Tony Neal
The Core DJs

I met Tony Neal back in the early 90s. He was quiet but effective. I was fresh out of prison and a little hot head. We met at CC's, a hangout for all the hustlers, players, pimps, robbers and killers. It was a death trap for all that hung out there. No bullshit, at least three people got shot or killed there every week. I didn't peep it then but Tony was a mastermind. He was the go-to DJ for all the flyest parties and he was a serious go-getter. I remember when I started doing all the big parties. Tony came up to me and said, "Man, how the fuck are you going to do a party and not have Tony Neal as your DJ?"

I was confused and thought, "Who the fuck does he think he is? I'm hiring Homer Blow from WNOV."

Tony was a big DJ in my hometown of Milwaukee, but Homer Blow was the DJ from the radio and if you booked him, you got a chance to get a free interview, which was free promotion. Tony was a member of a big organization so he was able to make a lot of human chess moves. Because of his contacts, he was able to open one of the biggest clubs in Milwaukee at the time. He called me and said, "I need you to come to my club, The City Club."

I said, "That's the biggest club in the Mil. That's your shit?"

He replied, "Yeah, nigga. Be there."

Tony never asked you to do something, he demanded that you do it. This was a good tactical move because it made Tony the

man amongst all the DJs in the city. I received another call from
Tony a few years later asking me to meet him in Miami. I told him I
would be there but some things came up and I couldn't make it.
Tony called me again and said, "Nigga, you missed it."

From that day on, Tony put together some of the coldest
chess moves I have ever seen. He formed The Core DJs, a group of
DJs that are recognized throughout the world. The Core DJs are
responsible for getting new music to the public for the labels and
entertainers. This was powerful because if you made music back
then, you wanted The Core DJs to play your music in the clubs and
on the radio. Tony had over four hundred DJs become a part of The
Core DJs from all over the world. Club DJs, radio DJs and even Big
Tigger, the host of BET's "Rap City" and "106 & Park."

Tony ran the game. The labels, rappers and the whole music
business were kissing his ass. Because of his boss chess moves,
Tony was getting top dollar just to sit on the board of these large
record labels. He was a master strategist. I'm sure he knew that
starting this movement of DJs would give him major power. He was
so powerful that he had artists that were asking $200K per show to
come to his club in Milwaukee, The Onyx, for free. I did some big
parties in the Mil but Tony was bringing big name artists to the town
every week. Akon put Tony on his team and made him apart of
Konvict Muzik. This all started from his first conference in Miami,
The Core DJ Retreat. This retreat is one of the largest retreats of its
kind and takes place in a different city every year all across
America. Rappers, labels, fans and anyone in the music business
attend the retreats.

The next time Tony called me was to do a party in Miami at
the world famous King of Diamonds. He booked my hotel at $500 a
night and I must admit that was one of the biggest parties I have
ever seen at KOD. Tony is a boss and I know for a fact that he
planned his moves like a chess player. I haven't talk to him in a few
years, but I was driving the other day in my 550 Benz listening to
Shade 45 and the DJ announced, "Ladies and gentlemen, welcome
back to Core DJ radio."

We are both from the same hood on Milwaukee's east side
and Tony is an east side boss. I saw this dude go from a hole in the

wall club DJ to one of the most powerful DJs in the world. People, human chess really works and the good thing about it is all you need is the secret: Game. If Tony's story doesn't inspire you and make you master the information in this book, this game, better known as human chess, is not for you.

Rob Owens
The Underground King of Skateboarding

The first time Rob and I kicked it in a bar, he acted like he didn't know anything about the game of pool. We played the first game and he was fucking up all over the place. I won. Then out of nowhere, he said he wanted to play for money. I said, "Hell yeah. What you got?"

Rob smiled and replied, "Let's play $20 a game. I'll break."

We racked the balls and started playing. His game was completely different this time around. He was shooting like a pro. This nigga got damn near every ball in. I couldn't believe I got hustled for my $20. At the end of the game, I looked at him and laughed. I asked, "How'd you learn to play?"

He replied, "I used to go to the pool hall on third and Vine with my dad back in the day. I played with him every day. I just liked hanging with my dad and the old school players."

"That's crazy. My dad used to take me there all the time, too. I bet they knew each other." Rob and I have been cool ever since.

Rob Owens is one of the best pro street street skaters in the skateboarding game. But that's not why I chose to feature him in this book. He is from my hometown, Milwaukee, WI, and Rob is full of game. When he was only seventeen, he started his first business venture printing T-shirts that he drew of a Black man sporting a huge fro with the logo *Black Skateboards* written on the shirt. Rob sold out of his T-shirts at his high school. This was just the beginning.

From that time on, Rob continued to skate and perfect his craft. Over the years, he plotted to be seen and gained local and national recognition and was featured in several magazines and kicked it with some of the most famous skateboarders the world has ever seen. Unfortunately, right when he was climbing the ladder of success, Rob took eleven bullets (total of fifteen from a previous shooting) and survived. Those shots put the skater out of commission for a few years.

While Rob was at home not skating, he was using his mind. Just when people started to count him out, he got back on his skateboard. He claimed that it was the only thing that gave him solace and helped him keep his sanity. Rob skated for a couple years to get his mojo back before he began competing again. Once he felt confident in his abilities after his body completely healed, he started planning and strategizing his new company called *Grime Official* where he built a team of skaters, most of whom he knew since he was a teenager. Rob now has a clothing line, skateboards, backpacks, stickers, sunglasses, wax and a whole bunch of other skateboard shit for sale with the *Grime Official* logo.

Rob has recently reconnected with one of his friends in Los Angeles, Chuck Deal, and they are planning a collaboration to flood America with *Grime Official* merchandise. This nigga even has me doing my own skateboard. That's right. Soon there will be a skateboard out with graphics from Pimpin' Ken. Skateboarding used to be stereotyped as a predominately White boy sport. Not anymore. Now you see the relationship between Hip Hop and skateboarding everywhere.

What impresses me most about Rob is that he never gave up. This man died nine times in the trauma center at Froedtert Hospital in Milwaukee and he still wouldn't put his skateboard down. When all the cards were stacked against him, he persevered like a boss human chess player. That's some real Milwaukee shit for your ass.

Big shout-out to Patrick Hergins and the other skaters of *Grime Official* who keep up with Rob's unique style of skating.

Reality Laster
The Jack of All Trades

When I first met my man Real, I thought he was Eazy-E the rapper from NWA. He had on all black and some very dark sunglasses and was driving a green and gold Bronco, very flashy. I remember asking people about him when I first came home from the joint. One dude that knew him was a rapper by the name of Ice Mone. He said that Real was the truth and he has been getting bread since he was sixteen years old. I was fresh out of prison, so I had to get to know all the players and the top dudes in the city. The fact that Reality was so young and respected made me watch homie for a minute.

One day I was in the check cashing place and I saw a flyer with Reality's face on it. He was promoting a show with Eazy-E. I said to myself, "Damn, this dude must have some real money to bring Eazy-E to Milwaukee." I went to the show and the people were more interested in Reality than Eazy-E. Girls were all over him and trying to get into his hotel room. He didn't tell me then but I was able to peep that he was putting down some real chess moves, because I would promote myself the same way a few years later. He also brought Tupac, Ice Cube and Dr. Dre to Milwaukee when he was big because there weren't any promoters fucking with rap like that back then. I was thinking to myself, "I'm going to have to work hard to out-chess this 'lil young player."

My aim was to be the top dog in the city and Reality was busting some big moves at only nineteen years old and he was in my way. Then out of nowhere, he was arrested for murder. That fucked me up because even though he was young, he was a smooth operator. He disappeared off the scene and I didn't see him until three years later.

Reality moved to Atlanta and had this bad Asian and Black mixed girl that was on some *Hustle and Flow* shit for him. She would go up to all the famous people and befriend them then she would introduce Reality as her cousin. She was working at the best club in Atlanta, *The Gentleman's Club*. This is where all the stars and athletes would go when they came to town. Reality, being the chess player he was, had her strategically working in the right place. She was so bad, I was trying to have her. I was in her ear every day. It must have been too much because Reality came out of hiding to greet me. He pulled up in a brand new green Range Rover and said, "Hey Pimpin' Ken. Let me talk to you."

I looked and looked again and I said, "Reality?"

He replied, "Yeah, man. It's me."

I got in his truck and he and I have been plotting and planning ever since. When I stepped foot into his big ass crib, I was shocked. I said, "Boy, what are you doing? Selling dope to all the strippers?"

He said, "Naw, man. They dropped the murder case and I packed up and moved to the A. Once I peeped the game, I put my girl in the strip club to get cool with the industry cats. That's been about a year ago and I now have a song with MC Breed, Too $hort and Ice-T."

He played the music for me and I said, "You're about to blow up now."

He said, "Ken, I've been reading this book call *The 48 Laws of Power* and I'm on some boss shit. In the last two years, I sold a hundred thousand records out of my trunk and I got my own money."

I said, "That's big, 'lil homie."

He said, "Not only that, I got this real estate game down. I'm making more money than all these rap cats. Fuck dealing with labels. I'm hiring the lawyers to do my deals. The same lawyers the big name rappers use like Andy Tavel and Jay Katriny."

I didn't call it human chess back then, but I thought, "This young dude has a lot of boss game."

He gave me the book *The 48 Laws of Power* and said, "Man, you're going to love this." I went home and read the book and fell in love with it. It was the first time someone that young had put me up on some real game.

Reality called me and asked me to come to one of his other houses. I walked in the house and there was a preppie-looking white woman sitting at the table. We went in the back and he told me, "That's the most powerful White woman in Hip Hop. She's the one that helped Cash Money records get their $100M deal."

I thought, "This guy has his girl working at the strip club meeting all the rappers, the most influential white woman in Hip Hop working the top flight lawyers and a real estate company to help him pay for all this. He is indeed a human chess player and I respect the fact that he was doing this slick shit way before I wrote this book. Hell, he gave me the book *The 48 Laws of Power*.

Reality eventually moved to Miami and made tons of money in real estate and has a $2M condo at the Trump Plaza with a studio built in his crib. We teamed up and are about to put together some serious chess moves. It's been years and we are both still plotting and planning like master chess players. He is a raw dude and I can assure you that my writing about him in this book was a part of his plan. The last time I talked to him was yesterday and we were in his studio working on an LP that will be available on iTunes very soon.

Reality has used human chess to become a successful man. He has bought Benz's, Bentley's and mansions. These things are hard to obtain but if you use your head and exploit every opportunity, you can make the same moves and acquire the same shit as Reality Laster. I use these human examples so you can see their come up and don't feel like it can't happen to you. You just have to use your mind and think of how you can get it done. In this book are many stories of how people did it. Study them, read between the lines and find the secrets.

Big Silk
The King of the Streets

My friend Big Silk is by far one of the fastest dudes I have come across in the street life. When we met, our first encounter was a battle of who could talk the slickest shit. I spit quick lines like, "Yeah, all I do is rest, dress and let my bitches do the rest. Sit at home, pick my toes and tell the dame to slide it under the door and get PK some more."

Silk laughed and replied, "Yeah, you can tell by my Rolls Royce that I'm a boss ho's choice so back up off me like the OJ's and spin up off me like the Barclays."

We went all night talking slick. So one day he said, "Let's go to the studio and have some friendly competition."

We went to the studio and spit game on the mic, roasting each other all night. Then I peeped that he wanted to use what we spit as a promotional tool. I said to myself, "This cat thinks he's slick. He's going to put the CD out and try to get some recognition off me." Nice chess move, but I doubled-back and told the engineer to scrap what we did because we were going to do it over. Silk asked the engineer to print him a CD of what we did and the engineer replied, "Pimpin' Ken told me y'all were going to rerecord it."

Silk looked at me and asked, "Man, why you do that?"

I smiled and replied, "Nice try, but I'm not going for that move, partner."

That was Silk for you, a master at the game of human chess. He was always plotting. One day Silk and I sat down and he said, "Man, I like what you're doing with the film game. I need you to show me that game."

I thought to myself, "Here he goes with that competition shit again." I replied, "Ok, I'll give you the game."

Unbeknownst to me, Silk had a plan and a strategy. He wanted to use the film game to reach disadvantaged youth. The first DVD he put out was called *The King of the Streets*. In this movie, he featured me, Snoop Dogg, Michael Vick and a lot of other stars. His purpose for this DVD was to speak to the youth and tell them to get out of the streets. He sold a lot of the movies and took the money and bought an office center where he raised money for his nonprofit organization.

Being a chess player, Silk changed his life and became a Minister. He produced four more films including one featuring the popular Mayor of Atlanta Shirley Franklin. Silk sold thousands more DVDs and this gave him some big time promotion. He now has the support of most of the community leaders and has a large compound where he feeds the hungry and helps the youth. He's a public speaker and speaks at the schools and prisons.

These are some very impressive chess moves from a former slick street player. I have to admit, I would have never expected Big Silk to be the positive dude he is now. When he asked me to show him the game, I was looking for him to be my competition but he was planning something way bigger. Now he's a leader and is playing chess on a huge level while sticking to a positive message and making an impact in the community. I'm happy to be a part of his life. Big Silk is one of the best human chess players out there.

Jayroll
Dying Breed Records Music

Earlier I wrote about my man JD making me CEO of his clothing store. We did that for a minute and moved on. I became one of the biggest pimps in America, then an intro and outro man for all the big name rap stars. But JD being the good dude he was saw how big rap was becoming and closed the store and let Jayroll turn it into a music studio.

Jayroll was the little homie. If you had a problem, he was the one you wanted to ride with you. He and JD had a relationship before me. Jay taught him how to get money and how to out-plot on the opposition. I really like Jayroll and I would pick him up and take him to all my dice games. I even took him to Chicago where I would get my dice made by an old player by the name of Honeyman.

One day we were riding and out of nowhere, he told me he's going to start a record label. At this time, young men from the hood were just starting to take their future into their own hands and become independent. Jayroll helped produce a group called the

County Boy Clique, including rappers Buck-0-Five and Baby Drew. This was one of the first rap cliques in Milwaukee and they were so good that they were out-selling all of the big name rappers. Baby Drew was a young slick talker from Chicago. What made Jayroll a boss player was he and his producer created a sound that Milwaukee could groove to.

Every time Buck-0-Five and Baby Drew would put out a song, the whole city would be singing the song. I asked Jayroll what his secret was and he replied, "Kenny, man, when I make music I want that quality sound. A sound that meets the industry standards. I'm not looking for a deal, the deal has to look for me."

I asked, "Ok, but don't you think you would do better with a major?"

He said, "Yeah and no. Yeah if you don't have a plan or strategy and you just want to be famous. No if you want all your money and you know how to sell music and *Dying Breed* knows how to sell music."

I'm not going to lie, this dude taught me a lot about ownership and being independent. That's why I produced my own DVDs and Jayroll would edit them for me. He would say, "Kenny, let me show you how to brand your product and sell it to retailers." He understood the psychology of the entertainment business. Even though his artists were local, in Milwaukee they were bigger than any national artist.

Jayroll's movement was so big, he became the go-to man for the Milwaukee Hip Hop scene. It was clever how he took a major approach to all his music and made everyone come to him to put their music out. Jayroll was smart and he saw how everyone was getting into independent videos so he educated himself on the video game by buying books on how to produce videos and complete the editing. By the end of that year, all independent videos were filmed by his new record label *Eye to Eye Records. Eye to Eye Records* became the biggest independent record company in the Midwest.

Jayroll hooked up with Porgie, a street dude with plenty of money. This was a wise chess move because Porgie helped Jayroll to get a lot of his projects started. I loved that my little homie was winning in the rap game. By this time, I was a somewhat of a national star. Jayroll called me and said, "Big homie, you're making some moves but you need that Milwaukee sound to follow you. You need that *Eye to Eye* sound."

I agreed, and Jayroll took my documentary *Pimpology* and laced it with that Baby Drew and *Country Boy* funk. To this day people ask me how to buy the music in *Pimpology*. What's crazy is that JD gave Jayroll the keys to his studio nineteen years ago and Jayroll is still that dude in Milwaukee, never selling out to the major record labels. If you are from Milwaukee and you're trying to get in the rap game, at some point you're going to run across Jayroll.

Jayroll is a master at human chess and he made it so people in Milwaukee that want to get into the rap game need him. I have to give it to him. He has made some serious money all the while making a name for himself and building his brand. He is one of the best chess players I have ever met. Jay has been busting some clever moves since he took over the store. I also want to give it up to Smalls, Ralph and Steve-O of *Infinite Records* who are responsible for Coo Coo Cal, the rapper from Milwaukee that had the hit song *In My Projects*.

Juanita Ivy
Simply My Mother

There is a large spot in my heart for my mother because I truly know that had she not had me, there would be no *Art of Human Chess: A Study Guide to Winning*. My mother used to say, "Boy, don't you play with me. I forget more than you know." Those words were profound to me because this suggests that she has been through a lot and I had a long way to go to get on her level.

My mother was from Tupelo, Mississippi and had a third grade education. She once told me that most of her classmates would drop out of school by the third grade and go work in the cotton fields. My mother worked in those same fields and by the time she was sixteen, she was married to my father and living on the south side of Chicago.

For the first few years of her marriage, she had four children and was a victim of domestic violence. My father would beat my mother mercilessly every day, sometimes twice a day. One day my big brother asked her, "Momma, why don't we leave and go where it's safe?" She looked at him and said, "Because I love y'all and I'll be damned if my kids grow up without a mother and a father like I did."

I was young but in my mind I thought this was the dumbest answer I ever heard. My father was not only abusive to my mother, he was also abusive to us. I was ready to go. My mother explained to me thirty-five years later why she stayed. She told me that my father had come from an abusive father and this was how he was raised to deal with life, but that he never showed her this side until they moved to Chicago. She said once she realized that, she devised a plan to keep her family together. She would cook him a plate so he would eat and go to sleep. She explained that my father would pass out every time she fed him and this would keep him from fighting with her.

She also told me how jealous he was. He would beat her if she just looked in the direction of a man. So my mother came up with strategies to stay home. Every time my father would ask her to go to the club with him, she would sniff onions and peppers so he would think she was sick. She knew that if she didn't go to the club, he would not accuse her of looking at other men.

My mother would sometimes leave and not call my father for a week, making him go crazy. She did this to put the thought in his head that if he didn't get his act together, he could lose his family. My father had thirteen brothers and sisters and he always believed that family was everything so my mother threatening to take his family away hurt him to his core.

I said to her, "Momma, can I put this story in my book *The Art of Human Chess: A Study Guide to Winning* because that's some serious psychology you were employing."

She replied, "Boy, I don't care. But let me tell you how I joined the church to really get him off my back. You see one thing I knew about your daddy is that he was scared of God and he knew better to hit a saved woman."

I interrupted her and asked, "Momma, you used God?"

She replied, "Yeah, at the time. But that was the best thing that happened to me because I got saved, sanctified and filled with the Holy Ghost."

My mother has now been in the church for over forty years and in that time before my father died in 2007, they may have had ten fights. My mother used to tell my father, "Fool, you better not put your hand on God's saint. You're going to go straight to hell." My father would look the other way and say, "Woman, you're crazy," but he would not hit her.

My mother can now read on a college level and has held every position of leadership in her church except pastor. She is one of the best chess players I have ever met. When my father died hitting my mom, he grabbed her and fell dead. My mother said my father's last words were, "Why you did this to me?" He then hit the floor. My mother is so real that she gave him a Presidential funeral, top of the line everything just to let all the haters know she stood by her man so she could save her kids.

Most of my siblings became businessmen and women and grew up loving our kids the same way my mother loved us. Had it not been for the human chess moves my mother made, this book may not have been written. Moms is married and her new husband opens doors, cooks for her and loves her to death. Momma, I love and salute you. May God continue to bless you. I love you too, Pops. If you read this, I know you're going to whoop my ass when we meet again.

THE BREAKDOWN

I have met a lot of boss players in my life. The first bosses I met were my parents. My mother taught me how to be patient and my father taught me a lot about the game. Coming from the same household, my brothers and sisters were full of game, too. I made it my business to surround myself with individuals who were game conscious like me.

161

I want to mention a few associates who have been impactful in my life. Valentino is a master of top game and has been clever enough to commute from city to city and still be recognized as a boss who has made some serious chess moves. International Slick from Tampa is a young nigga coming up as a master at human chess. King Napoleon has been successful in intertwining the game with the business world. He uses his street knowledge to get him into the corporate world, but at the same time employs human chess tactics to further his success in the business world.

My man Drez So Digital has mastered the game of human chess and is an A-List producer in the city of Milwaukee. I admire how he got cool with my brother Marvin and then respectfully was introduced to me. He helped me with my son, KP's, music and now we're on the same team. I'm managing him and his music career. That was a cold move, Drez. You got me on your team, partner. You are officially a human chess player.

I have had a lot of people cross me over the years, but never those closest to me. The same associates I have are the ones that have been around me since I was a teenager. We grew together and complimented each other. Flock with feathers like your own. You can't fly as an eagle with feathers from a crow.

Chess Notes

Chapter Eighteen
The Greatest Human Chess Players of All Time

"In life you will have gains and losses, successes and failures. What determines your fate is how you handle them."

~Excerpt from:
Pimpin' Ken and Karen Hunter
Pimpology/The 48 Laws of the Game
Published by Simon & Schuster~

"A clever man commits no minor blunders."
~Goethe~

This chapter describes some of the greatest human chess players of all time and some of the strategies that they used in order to execute their plans. The individuals that I have chosen to represent in this chapter have proven themselves as masters of human chess based on their maneuvers. These examples and applications will give you real life experiences of those who played the game from all genres such as politics, business, entertainment, activism, and entrepreneurship.

Reverend Dr. Martin Luther King, Jr.
The Consummate Strategist

One thing a lot of people don't understand is that the Civil Rights Movement had some of the bravest and most strategic individuals fighting for their freedom that our time has ever seen. They plotted, planned and deceived their racist opposition. There were secret meetings between the Civil Rights leaders and government officials. President John Fitzgerald Kennedy and Reverend Dr. Martin Luther King, Jr. worked together to end the injustice of that time. Kennedy and King understood that to get certain laws passed, they had to be tactful and strategic devising plans to get their policies passed.

One move they plotted was when they ordered the State of Alabama to allow Vivian Malone and James Hood to attend the University of Alabama. Kennedy and Martin both knew that they were going to receive opposition because the Governor of Alabama was a racist and he would shout, "Segregation now, segregation tomorrow, segregation forever!" They used his ass as a pawn because they had already planned to send national guards down there to overthrow his power. So when he stood at the door trying to block Malone and Hood from entering into the college, he made himself look like a damn fool. Kennedy used the experience of a Governor standing at a door to education blocking two black students as an opportunity to address the nation about Civil Rights in America. Governor George Wallace didn't know they were using him as a pawn in a larger game of chess.

That same night, President Kennedy appeared on television and gave his Civil Rights Address. Game is for real and I tell you if you're not sharp, you will be set up to be played. This human chess game is deep. Right after Kennedy addressed the nation, Dr. King sent Kennedy a telegram saying, "It was one of the most eloquent, profound and unequivocal pleas for justice and freedom of all men ever made by any President." They were on some player shit working behind closed doors making big shit happen.

Martin Luther King, Jr. was a clever chess player and plotted his every move. When Rosa Parks refused to go to the back of the bus and give up her seat to a White person, Martin led the boycott. Even though he was only twenty-seven at the time, he knew this was going to be a move that would lead him to the legend he is today. Just think, Rev. Dr. Martin Luther King, Jr. has a street named after him in almost every major city, his own national holiday, centers named after him, and a statue in Washington, D.C. next to President Lincoln. There is no man in America that played the human chess game better Reverend Dr. Martin Luther King, Jr.

Another clever move he made to forward the cause of Blacks in America was when he set the bigots up to sick the dogs on those kids. Kennedy called MLK and said, "I need something big to take before congress to push this Civil Rights Act."

King replied, "Watch the news." Martin told the people to go to work and let the children protest. He did this because he understood that a racist mind had no rationality and given the opportunity, it would respond irrationally every time. And that's exactly what happened. The racist police attacked their dogs on

167

innocent children while the whole world was watching. Martin Luther King, Jr. outfoxed them and made them look like cold-hearted, inhumane people that were full of hate.

Kennedy called King and said, "That's exactly what I needed."

The movement was about boss moves and at the end of the day, they made shit happen. After Kennedy was assassinated, King became cool with President Lyndon Johnson and on July 2nd, 1964 in Washington D.C., President Lyndon Johnson reached to give MLK one of the seventy-two pens used to sign the Civil Rights Act of 1964: Checkmate. Just sit back and let this resonate for a minute. If it wasn't for the human chess moves of Rev. Dr. Martin Luther King, Jr., President Barack Obama may not have been the first Black President. If you master human chess, you may be able to change the world.

Fortunately, as I write about the great chess moves that Rev. Dr. Martin Luther King, Jr. employed, I decided to go to the theater and see the critically acclaimed *Selma*, which is a movie based on the march from Selma to Montgomery, AL. As a clever chess player, I decided to research Martin's move of turning around at that bridge. I found out that he and Lyndon B. Johnson had arranged a secret meeting in which King agreed to turn around and Johnson would give all Americans the right to vote, an act he signed shortly after the march from Selma. During Johnson's speech, he quoted Dr. King saying, "We shall overcome." These words were powerful to all involved in the civil rights movement.

These facts are very pivotal to this piece. The movie sparked Barack Obama to allocate $50M for restoration in preparation for the 50th anniversary of the Voting Rights Act. What is so profound about this is that Martin Luther King's chess moves, which were employed over fifty years ago, are now checkmating the children of the bigots of their time.

Barack Obama
President of the United States of America

Ladies and gentlemen, I present to you the first Black President of the United States of America, Barack Hussein Obama. What is there to say about a Black man that worked on the gang infested south side of Chicago and got the richest Black woman in the world to get off her rich ass and campaign for him (yes, I'm talking about Oprah Winfrey) other than he's a boss player. I don't know if he planned that shit, but it looks damn good.

As far as his Presidential campaign is concerned, he planned and plotted that shit like a master human chess player. One good sign of a master is that he plans months, if not years, down the road, because he must win and crush his opponent with brute force. Barack Obama outfoxed everyone that was in his way to become President of the United States, including the Democratic Party. Normally in the Party, they have what is called a preempted nominee and that year it was Hillary Clinton. She had the name, contacts, supporters and millions of dollars backing her. There was no way anyone was going to beat her unless there was a miracle from God himself. No one anticipated that her opponent would be a master human chess player with boss game for that ass.

The first chess move Obama made was to set up an office in Iowa. He did this because he knew that if he won Iowa, the media would take him seriously and give him a lot of free press, increasing his popularity. He campaigned for an entire year, reaching out to the people of Iowa on a regular basis. He did this so that when it was time to select the Democratic nominee, Barack Obama's name would be as big as Hillary's and the rest of them. This was smart because it was repetition at its best. The media was helping to brainwash the public with the name Barack Obama.

Another thing he did was get with Mark Zuckerberg, the young creator of one of the number one social media sites in the

169

world, Facebook. They devised a plan where he could raise millions of dollars at $20-200 a pop. Doesn't seem like a lot of money, but when you get $20 from five million people, it adds up pretty quickly. Facebook had hundreds of millions of people and Zuckerberg gave Obama access to all of them.

Money rules in politics and normally the rich boys put up millions of dollars and basically buy the Presidency. Obama had the people's money and no one to tell him how to spend it. He spent big money in Iowa on his campaign and won. It was an upset. Obama knew Hillary would step up her game and win New Hampshire. But what Hillary and the Democratic Party didn't know was that the show was on. Obama, being a constitutional lawyer, knew that a tie would mean that all states would come into play. And being the clever chess player that he is, Obama had set up campaign offices in most of these states. He was light years ahead of Hillary and by the time her staff realized how clever he was, it was too late. He was fucking her up in the polls and the media was all over him. The funny thing about the shit was that Obama planned it all the way to the end.

Obama is very intelligent and he knew they were going to bring everything his way. He just continued to outfox them, never becoming the angry Black man, preaching change and winning White people over to his side. This was fucking the Democratic Party up. What was going on? I figured it out and I'm just a Black man from Milwaukee, WI. Plainly, Obama and his camp were playing chess and Hillary's team was playing checkers.

After he beat Hillary, he raised millions more and went overseas and met with Heads of State and the media followed him everywhere he went making him look like a rock star. This was a clever move because even though he'd had no experience in foreign policy, he still looked like an American President meeting with all of those big boys overseas. Every move he made was classic and when he got back to the United States, he was too famous and the Republicans didn't stand a chance.

The media loved him. He made them money because every time he was on TV, people would watch just to see what this master chess player was going to do next. His next move was brilliant. The campaigns, debates and bullshit were all over and out of nowhere, Obama spent most of the millions he had left to buy an hour on all the major networks to make it look like he was giving a State of the Union Address. The opposition was shocked at this move because they never saw it coming.

Once he was in office, he had to keep busting moves. The Republicans refused to work with him so he went to the CEOs of the larger corporations. He had them help him get the economy back on track, gave them access to the White House and took pictures with them. This means a lot to those power heads, and Obama is a smart enough chess player to understand that.

David Axelrod, Robert Gibbs and Barack Obama went on to win a second term, once again outfoxing Obama's opponent and all of his critics. Study this dude carefully and you will see what playing human chess is all about. His game is on ten and I've never seen anyone that plays the game like Obama. His moves and life are the blueprint for one to master the game and do it for real.

The first time I ever voted in my life was for Barack Obama, and they told me when I was little that we would never see a Black President. Never say never, especially to a master human chess player. When we get through with your ass, you won't know what hit you. Barack was and is a master strategist and he was able to see Iowa as the prize, raise money in small numbers from millions of Americans and ultimately use the media to become famous as fuck to the point where White America loved him like they loved Elvis. You have to give it to him. He is one of the greatest human chess players of all time.

Barack Obama really is a master at the game. While vesting the Pope, he got in the Pope's ear and asked him to let the Cuban government know that he is willing to normalize the relationship between the governments. This was in 2013 and by the end of 2014 after many secret meetings with the Pope and the Cuban government, Obama got the Cubans to release an aid worker and agree to a better relationship. What's significant about this is that it was the first time in fifty-three years that the US had been able to talk to the Cubans. What made this a slick chess move is that it was done in secrecy and Obama didn't say shit until the deal was done.

Obama's best move was in the beginning of his first Presidential term when he hired his former opponent, Hillary Clinton, as his Secretary of State and sent her around the world as his diplomatic pawn. This was smart because it guaranteed she would not run against him in his second term. Barack Obama could kick his feet up, lean back with his arms crossed and confidently say, "Checkmate!"

Nelson Mandela
The Human Pawn

There are many examples of leaders being clever and strategic, but there are few leaders that made the sacrifice that Nelson Mandela made. Yes, leaders will plot and plan from their boardrooms and talk to government officials and other leaders about the plight of their people. But few have given their freedom for twenty-seven years as a human pawn for the freedom and liberation of their fellow countrymen.

Mandela is a hell of a chess player because even though he was a prominent South African with degrees and a well known boxer, he gave all that up and joined the movement. He was so vocal that the Whites of South Africa wanted him dead or alive and labeled him a terrorist. His only crime was fighting for justice for the people. He knew dead or alive that he would impact the movement because he was passionate and popular. That was a sacrifice he was willing to make. He kept protesting against the Apartheid and was eventually taken into custody. That's where he piloted his strategy.

He had his wife at the time, Winnie, tell his story to the world. How can a prominent Black South African be incarcerated for fighting for democracy and the liberation of his people? History is filled with examples of the oppressed wanting to be freed from their oppression. She took his message to Cuba, Europe, South

America, the Middle East and the United States. She reached out to athletes, musicians, actors and political leaders everywhere. People felt the message. His people organized boycotts and sanctions aimed at the removal of the Apartheid system. Mandela made himself larger than life from a jail cell.

This was some clever shit because he became the King and the piece on the human chessboard that everyone in the world wanted to protect. He was eventually freed and became the President of South Africa. Let the boss game continue. Every White South African was wondering how he was going to govern. Being that he was a master human chess player, he did the opposite of what everyone thought.

Mandela was fair in his decisions and gave them equal power even though they were the minority. This shocked them. How could an innocent man that just spent twenty-seven years of his life in prison be so generous? Mandela was a master at the game and he knew the course was larger than him. It was about the future of his country. Mandela then went on a world tour and met with the Heads of State everywhere and had the sanctions lifted. His country began building and the children could now grow up free of Apartheid, a peace they had never felt. Mandela was a very skilled planner and strategist. He was also a gentle, patient man who always remained non-threatening and non-violent.

He had one more thing to do before he had his checkmate. Mandela used the 1995 Rugby World Cup, which was held in South Africa, as an opportunity to bring Blacks and Whites together. Black South Africans hated the national rugby team, the Springboks, because they represented Apartheid. Despite resistance from Black South Africans, Mandela supported the Springboks and through strategic moves on his part, Blacks came to enthusiastically cheer for the team. After South Africa won the game, Mandela put on the Springboks jersey and cap and walked on the field. The White South Africans were in shock. Then out of nowhere, they began to shout, "Mandela, Mandela, Mandela!" South Africa's national team, the Springboks represented the wickedness of Apartheid. His security was worried because they didn't know what to expect. Then smiles appeared on their faces in adoration for their leader. This brought the people closer and once again Mandela checkmated his opponents.

Power was not what Mandela wanted. He wanted his people liberated and he gave twenty-seven years of his life as proof of his dedication to his beliefs. Now that's some human chess for that ass. Like I said many times throughout this book, it takes game, planning, maneuvering, tactics, deception and patience to play human chess. Be like Mandela and get that shit done even if you have to use yourself as a pawn.

Oprah Winfrey
The Billionaire Queen

There are going to be some of you that say how can you say that Oprah is clever and she thinks like all those powerful men you talk about in this book? In my opinion, she exemplifies and embodies all of the components of a great chess player. Let's take a look. From the time Oprah opened up to the world and let us know she was a victim of abuse, we all fell in love with her. The majority of White and Black women have been in situations where they were victims of rape or abuse, so when Oprah went public with it she became the face of all those that were abused. I don't know if she planned it like that, but it was a very clever move because here you had one of the most intelligent Black women in the world with an audience of millions and they all sympathized with her.

What America wasn't ready for was how smart she was. Oprah ran with it and she became one of the largest talk show hosts in the game. She won people over, set trends and became the go-to lady in relationships, family matters and current affairs. She started the Oprah Book Club which was so powerful that if you could get her to say your book on the Oprah show, it became an instant bestseller and you would make millions overnight. This was powerful because everyone had to kiss her ass and they dare not say anything bad about her because she could end a career. The show got so big that she made the network give her more money.

What people didn't know was that she was playing chess all along and setting herself up to surpass all of her bosses. Her first clever chess move was fucking with Dr. Phil, a middle-class White doctor that was basically a replica of Oprah. But the brilliant thing about this was it made men come on board because for a long time, Oprah was considered to be for the ladies. Dr. Phil gave Oprah that CEO status she needed. Before that she was just this rich talk show host.

She then extended her brand by positioning her friend Gayle King in other networks. Everyone knows that wherever you see Oprah, you see Gayle. With Gayle being on the radio and TV, Oprah was also there. Now she was really powerful and within a few years became the first African-American billionaire. Money talks and boy did her money talk.

She strategized her next move. Dr. Oz, an upper-middle class White man, would basically become the on-air doctor for most Americans. This guy would break down medical situations where a baby could understand, and then give home remedies to the viewing audience. This was a classic and an instant hit. Oprah was on a roll and was running circles around her competition. She had positioned herself as the undisputed champion of hosting.

Her next move was to test her hand a little more. She won White men over, became the first African-American billionaire, was one of the most power people on Earth and proved that she can make other talk show stars as well as turn any book into an instant bestseller. Now she wanted to assist in electing our first Black President. She put on her campaign shoes and helped the first Black man get elected into the Presidency, Barack Obama. She knew she had the people in her hand and it was time to put the checkmate in play.

She bought her own network, properly named OWN (Oprah Winfrey Network). The crazy thing about it was that it looked like it was going to be a family network and that she would be of little competition to the other networks that had the wild and crazy shit. At first, it didn't look so good for her and I wasn't sure she would be successful in this new endeavor. Then out of nowhere, she started producing crime stories and having gangster rappers like 50 Cent on there. She appeared with Jay-Z drinking quarter water in the hood. All of a sudden, her ratings went up and she was competition for the large networks. They never saw her coming. They thought she was too conservative and out of touch, but Oprah fooled them all and checkmated the television game once again.

Donald Trump
The Ruthless Real Estate Tycoon

Donald Trump is the most ruthless and organized human chess players of all time. He is very strategic and has a patience level that is matched by few. He was busting moves way back in his twenties. One of the most clever moves he made was when he met with the owners of General Electric (GE) and negotiated the purchase of the Commodore Hotel located by Grand Central Station in New York City, now properly renamed Trump Tower International. Before they considered selling, Trump came up with a bunch of game about how he was going to better the neighborhood and create jobs. GE promised Trump that he could have the building.

Trump then went to the city and told them that if they gave him a tax break, he would fix the decaying building and bring jobs to the city. They agreed. Then GE switched up and told Trump he had to bid like everyone else. Trump agreed because he knew the other developers didn't have the game on what to do with a big project. Trump wanted to renovate it into a luxury hotel. So as a clever human chess player, he brought the Hyatt on board so he could use their experience. But the president of the Hyatt really didn't want to fuck with Trump like that because he was only twenty-seven years old. So Trump went and hired a sixty year old dude that was a respected real estate broker. This dude was just a pawn. Trump was the King and a master at manipulation.

Donald Trump's strategies worked. The Hyatt came on board

176

and Trump put down some of the best game New York has ever seen. He approached the city and told them that the Hyatt won't fuck with New York anymore unless they give them a tax break. The city agreed and gave Trump a forty year tax break, a deal that everyone came up on. Trump bought the Commodore for $10M and paid the city $6M in back taxes. He then sold the hotel to the city for $1. The city agreed to lease it back to Trump for ninety-nine years. The banks financed that deal with the quickness. As a matter of fact, one of the banks was across the street because they knew real estate in that hood was going to go up big time. This was a masterful move from Trump. He brought businesses to the area and that increased the value of the neighborhood.

In chess, it is advised to plan ten steps ahead, but Trump planned this shit fifty steps ahead. His game was not transparent and they never saw this twenty-seven year old boss coming. If you read any of Trump's books, they read like a commercial. He has never stopped running game or promoting himself. What businessman do you know before Trump that had a reality show about them taking care of business? *The Apprentice* was so successful that it ran for a few seasons and was good as hell. What made it a good chess move is millions of people were tuning in to the Trump brand and Trump was getting paid for the shit.

Donald Trump is very clever. When Mike Tyson was larger than life and was selling out Vegas, Trump befriended my idol, Don King. Next thing people knew, they were going to Atlantic City to see Mike Tyson fight and Trump Casinos were banking like a motha fucka. If you look at the videos of King and Trump, you would think Trump was from the hood. He reached out to all the A-list African-Americans and invited them to his casinos. He was often spotted with P-Diddy and other rappers. Can you imagine this billionaire hanging with thugs? Don King was a convicted murderer, but Trump didn't give a fuck. He was playing chess and making millions.

To me, Trump is a real boss. He doesn't let anything get in his way. The only time I've seen him out of character is when he tried to go against Barack Obama. He was mad at Obama about something and was trying to say Obama was not a citizen. Other than that, he's a bad MF.

Jay-Z
The Consummate Businessman

I picked Shawn "Jay-Z" Carter because he is one of the most clever dudes in the game when it comes to strategizing and plotting on his opponent, and game recognizes game. The way he thinks is crazy to me because he wins most of the human chess games he plays.

The first example I will give is when he and his CEO, Damon Dash, got into it. I would pick up the magazine and Dame would be talking shit like a motha fucka and I was thinking, "Shit, I know Jay is going to say something back." He never did. He was too clever for that. He was setting Dame up for the big payback. Somehow they ended up in LA Reid's Def Jam office selling Rocafella records for a few million. That seems fair, right? What Dame didn't know was that Jay had strategized the whole move. As soon as the deal was over, Jay was president of Def Jam and the sole owner of Rocafella records. That's right. They gave him the company back for free. Brilliant chess move. Dame never saw it coming and wasn't able to anticipate the checkmate.

Jay-Z is a master of the buildup and capitalizes on game. His patience is not to be compared to anyone in Hip Hop. Another clever move was his endorsement of Cristal. He built them up to be the top champagne in the world only to bring them down and move on to a brand that he eventually made millions off of.

Legend has it that the boy Hov was in a shop one day and came across some new shit called Ace of Spade. He liked it and put it in the *Show Me What You Got* video. But those of us who are also clever know better. This is what I found out. Jay hooked up with this company that had ties to this family in France that was selling this shit called Antique Gold which costs roughly $13 to make but sells at about $60 a bottle. This was a deal set up by imported brands where Jay-Z received millions of dollars, but Jay will never admit this because he is a chess player that will never let his opponent figure him out. All I heard is that they move thousands of bottles a year and Jay gets a piece of that. Cristal was ultimately dead. Jay-Z now gets all that paper they were getting. This was a master move because they never saw him coming and it was well planned out.

Another clever chess move was when he got with Ratner, a high rise developer who was one of the perspective buyers of the Nets at the time. Jay was plotting all the time, setting up his next move. He became part owner of the team but his real move, which was planned five moves down the road, was to bring the Nets to Brooklyn. This was live because he and a few investors had bought property where the stadium was going to be built and now that shit is worth millions. Not to mention Jay is from Brooklyn and has a lot of fans in those areas of the town. You have to love the way Jay thinks. He is a master at human chess and embodies all the qualities it takes to continue checkmating any opponent who feels strong enough to be his opposite.

It is said that Jay invested $1M in the Nets, and in 2014, he made about $8M profit. But the clever thing is that he is now a sports agent and all the top flight athletes want to sign with your boy. The first deal he closed was for $240M for a fucking baseball player. This cat is the epitome of the principle of human chess. It's simple, people. It's a thinking man's game.

One last thing, in my opinion, is that Jay checkmated the industry when he married Beyoncé and laced her with the game. In the last month of 2013, she released her album on iTunes with no marketing, no promotion or anything. The best human chess move ever. Why? Because right before our very eyes, Beyoncé released the album on social media creating a frenzy with her fans as well as the media. The media talked about the album for a week straight, giving her free publicity. She sold over a million copies that week and we have to remember these were all downloads. That means there was very little cost involved in launching the project, resulting in mostly profit. And at about $20 an album, she made damn near $30M in the first couple weeks. Jay-Z is the man and I take my hat off to this master chess player.

50-Cent
The Underdog that Overcame

GGGG-Unit! That's right. 50 Cent is the creator of the G-Unit brand. I say brand because that's exactly what he did. He branded G-Unit into a multi-million dollar enterprise. How did he do it and what makes him a master at human chess? First, I want to point you to a book that is one of my personal favorites, 50's book *The 50th Law*. In this book, 50 and Robert Greene, the author of the bestseller *The 48 Laws of Power*, lay out 50's life and his struggles in Jamaica, Queens and how using common sense mixed with street knowledge got him through those mean streets.

One of the slickest moves 50 made was to make a record that details him robbing everyone in the music industry. Although this was some street shit, it was brilliant. It was a perfect chess move because it had the entire music industry saying, "Who is this 'lil nigga talking about robbing us?" What came out of it was a record deal with Columbia Records.

50 was busting some real clever chess moves, but he had famous opponents like Rapper Ja Rule and CEO Irv Gotti. They were also playing chess, blocking 50's every move. It was alleged that they were responsible for 50 losing his deal with Columbia Records.

Ultimately, 50 got shot nine times. When this happened, he fell back and began to play chess on another level. He came up with an idea for G-Unit and a masterful plan to get it started. The first thing he did was hire a lawyer that had ties to platinum rapper Eminem's lawyer, Paul Rosenburg. This was game at its highest level because it was not transparent and 50 never personally asked Em for a deal. 50's lawyer, Theodore Sedlmayr, gave Em's lawyer a copy of 50's mix tape and Rosenburg gave it to Em. What makes this a clever chess move is that 50 hired a lawyer that knew and was good friends with Em's lawyer. Everyone trusts their lawyer and accepts their advice. Plus 50 sold his lawyer on the idea that they both stood to make big money if it goes down, and they did.

Once 50 had the deal, he put his next chess move into play. He put G-Unit everywhere. Go to YouTube.com and look at the *Wanksta* video and you will see a big booty chick wearing a G-Unit sweat suit with G-Unit printed on her fat ass. Finally, the album comes out and 50 says G-Unit about a hundred times in the album.

Next, a G-Unit shoe deal between 50 and Reebok was born. Because of these smaller accomplishments, 50 was able to start G-Unit clothing, G-Unit Records and G-Unit books, which further enhanced the umbrella of his business. The album sold 12M copies worldwide and even 50 knew that Eminem played a part in his success. The Em connection made 50 Cent a household name and one of the largest brands in the Hip Hop community.

50, being a master of chess, knew that his psychology and reputation was strong enough to invest in something outside of Hip Hop, Vitamin Water. He made $100M from that deal and became richer than Eminem. You have to give 50 Cent his credit. Here's a street dude that came from the slums of Queens, NY and became one of the richest Black men in America. He outfoxed his lawyer, Em's lawyer and Em. All while helping them to get richer, which was a win in the end for everyone.

Em was signed to one of the best producers we have ever seen, Dr. Dre, so 50 got platinum beats that helped him sell all those records. He slipped the word G-Unit in that album over and over, brainwashing the public to his brand. He made millions and even helped his artists go platinum. Young Buck and Lloyd Banks both sold millions and Tony Yayo sold 900,000 on house arrest. 50 is one clever human chess player and this is why I chose his experiences and his tactfulness to be portrayed and included in *The Art of Human Chess: A Study Guide to Winning.*

The most powerful thing 50 did was to make the people think that there was no way G-Unit would ever come back together and then out of nowhere, he brings G-Unit out at the Summer Jam 2014. This is how game works. You must let your opponent sleep. Don't wake them up. Plot, plan and strategize on their ass and then smile about it.

Now y'all know why he threw that baseball pitch the wrong way. Peep how much free publicity he got from that move. Slick dude. You go 50.

Dr. Dre
The Quiet Storm

I don't know Dr. Dre personally like I know a lot of the other people in the entertainment business, but I have studied his career over the years and I must say he is a very impressive human chess player. He's a master player, but he doesn't flaunt it. He just moves and you will never know what he did until he has a finished product. Then you think to yourself, "Damn, Tupac, Eminem and 50 Cent sold ten million records?" Yes, Dre is responsible for some of the biggest acts in the game. Every rapper in Hip Hop wants a Dr. Dre beat. When I was hanging around rappers, they would say to me, "Ken, if I ever get a Dre beat, it's a wrap."

Dr. Dre is a master chess player. He has built a career on rapping and producing beats for some of the best and most recognized rappers the Hip Hop game has ever heard. He, like 50 Cent, knew that after all of those years of building himself up in the music industry, he was strong enough to make a deal that would put him on the next level. He came out with *Beats by Dre*. You may not get a record produced by him, but you can get his headphones. This was beyond brilliant because he brought his genius as a tangible item into the household of millions. The last time I checked, these headphones grossed billions of dollars and the makers of *Beats by Dre* gave Dre a check for $300M, which gave him a number three spot on Forbes alongside Puffy and Jay-Z.

Dr. Dre and Jimmy Iovine, co-founder of Interscope Records, understood that they would get all the stars to wear Beats by Dre for free and this would boost the sales of the headphones with very little marketing dollars. Although Dre does rap, he only puts out a record every ten years so he's not a threat to other rappers. He really is though, and 50 Cent was the first one to peep game. In 50's mind, Dre was getting all this money and rappers were making him richer through their endorsements. This is more than likely why Dre let 50 out of his record deal. Dre is the type of human chess player that creeps up on you and you will never see him coming.

Years ago, the CEO of Death Row Records showed up at Dr. Dre's house demanding that Dre give up all his masters. Dre gave Suge Knight all of the masters. But what people didn't know was that Dre had a plan. He gave Suge those masters because he had already established Aftermath Records. From Aftermath Records, Dre brought us the Chronic which sold millions, Eminem, Eve, 50 Cent, Game, and Kendrick Lamar. We're talking over a billion in sales right there. Now I hear Dre is coming out with Beat Music. This is big because he is smart enough to ride that horse. *Beats by Dre* is successful so let's let the next move be an even bigger move.

There is a lot I can say about Dr. Dre, but I think this brief synopsis will showcase his human chess skills and prove he is a master of the game. Dr. Dre gave out custom headsets to the stars, including a deal he struck with LeBron James to give him a stake in the company that net LeBron $30M from the sale to Apple. Once he made the deal, he showed up on YouTube with R&B singer Tyrese talking big shit. He screamed, "I'm the first Hip Hop billionaire and I'm from the west coast!" Yes, Dr Dre is Hip Hop's billionaire. The deal with Apple for $3.2B made him the King of the game. Checkmate, Hip Hop world.

Magic Johnson
The Ultimate Human Chess Player

There has never been a player in the game of basketball like Magic Johnson. When you saw him pass the ball, you knew he planned and strategized his moves. I used to hear his teammates say shit like, "Man, when Magic has the ball you have to keep your eyes on him." He maneuvered through the locker room like he was a happy kid. What his teammates didn't know was how much of a cold calculating human chess player Magic was and is.

For example, when Kareem injured his leg, Magic came in the locker room and said, "Have no fear, Magic is here." He gave them a pep talk and out of nowhere, he announced that he would be taking Kareem's place as center. They looked at him like he was crazy, but Magic was a human chess player and he knew this would confuse the 76ers, who at that time were led by none other than Julius Erving, AKA Dr. J. Magic played center and won his first championship at age nineteen and became the biggest star in the NBA.

Magic also knew that the Black and White tension was still crazy, so he created an illusion that he and Larry Bird were in this fierce fight for supremacy. The best White player in the world vs. the best Black player in the world. This was all game. They loved each other because they made each other better. But what was smart about the rivalry was that it made White people cheer for Bird, Black people cheer for Magic and made the NBA, as well as both of them, rich as hell.

Magic was an excellent and clever businessman so he knew that in the long run this would help him advance in business. Everyone was talking about Bird and Magic, making the Magic brand larger than life. Magic eventually contracted the AIDS virus and his basketball career was over.

This didn't stop Magic at all. He just let his next move be his best move and he plotted his way to become the national spokesperson for AIDS. Very strategic because now he is the face of the biggest epidemic the world has seen. He immediately went strong on his business endeavors. He saw an opportunity to invest in the urban community and he opened up Magic Johnson Theaters in the ghettos of major cities. This was not only a good chess move, but a creative way to build his brand. Magic's investment in theaters made him enough money to invest in Starbucks and Magic's TGI Fridays. He used the success of the theaters to convince the owner of Starbucks to not only put Starbucks in the hood, but he also retained fifty percent ownership of the venture.

Magic had his eyes on a much larger prize and all of his maneuvers were to set him up for what was to come in his near future. The Magic Johnson Foundation raised $300M in its first two years and $600M six months after. It is reported that the Foundation at one time raised over a $1B in a matter of days. Hell of a human chess move, using other people's money to get rich. Magic is still alive after having been diagnosed with the deadly disease over twenty years ago and is now worth $500M. He is one of the best human chess players of all time because he played the game even when it looked like it was over for him and won.

RIP to my little brother, Elijah Ivy, who died of HIV-related complications in 2007. I dedicate this chapter to him. I know he's in heaven saying checkmate, my brother just mentioned me with the great Earvin "Magic" Johnson.

Sylvester Stallone
The Underdog

Sylvester "Sly" Stallone has an unbelievable story. He was completely broke with $106 in his bank account and lived in a 1 ½ bedroom apartment with his wife and six month old son that they rented for $215 a month with roaches in the kitchen and a punching bag in the living room. Stallone even sold his dog for $50 because he was so broke. But Sly was a master at human chess and like any master, he had a plan.

After watching the championship fight in 1975 between Chuck Wepner and Muhammad Ali, Sly was inspired. He said to himself, "Let's talk about stifled ambition and broken dreams and people who sit on the curb looking at their dreams go down the drain." He thought about it for a month, which he calls his inspiration stage. I call this preparation for the checkmate that is to come.

Sly did not act on his thoughts just yet. For the next ten months, he claims he allowed his thoughts to incubate. After this incubation stage, Stallone picked up a pen and in what he calls the verification stage, wrote *Rocky* in 3 ½ days. Sly would get up at 6 A.M. and write the screenplay by hand. His wife, Sasha, would type his words. They worked as a team to get *Rocky* completed and ready to sell to the big name Hollywood producers. Sly had one condition, that he and only he play the character "Rocky."

Hollywood was very interested in Sylvester Stallone's script. The bidding reached $265K, but Sly executed extreme patience and refused to sell unless he could play the lead role. The money men all wanted a big named actor to play "Rocky," but Sly was adamant in starring in the movie. "I never would have sold it," he claimed. "I'd rather bury it in the backyard and let the caterpillars play 'Rocky.'"

Sylvester Stallone's extreme patience, plotting and planning finally paid off. He got his way and sold his script to producers Irwin Winkler and Robert Chartoff who allowed him to star in his own movie *Rocky*. Some of his family members were also involved in the project taking roles such as the timekeeper in a fight scene and a street corner singer. Even his dog, that he bought back for $3K, starred in the movie.

Rocky has earned ten Academy Award nominations, including two for Best Actor and one for Best Original Screenplay. And to think, this movie almost did not grace the movie theaters had Sly not been persistent and patient. Sly is an ultimate human chess player. He exhibited extreme patience even when it financially hurt him and his family, which is very difficult to do. He waited to get the right deal because he never wanted to sell out. He was rejected 1500 times when he was trying to sell his movie to producers but he never gave up.

Sly is a true underdog who overcame adversity. He believed in himself and his body of work. The big producers wanted an actor that everyone was familiar with. But Sly was so passionate about his film, he knew that only he could embody the character of "Rocky" completely and connect with the audience on a personal level.

I salute Sylvester Stallone for refusing to relinquish his creativeness and sell out simply for money. He waited for the deal that he knew was right and look what happened. Sly went on to star in other movies including the series *Rambo,* which also became a huge success. *Rocky* is one of the greatest film series of all time grossing over $1B at the worldwide box office, checkmate.

Being patient and staying true to yourself really does pay off in the end. Never sellout to anyone or anything that goes against your principles. Be patient and you will outfox your opponent in the end. All great human chess players practice the art of being patient. It can mean the difference between getting on and falling off.

Kim Kardashian
The Calculated Diva

Out of all of the people I wrote about in this chapter, Kim is the most elusive human chess player I have ever seen. She plays human chess, but she possesses a quiet style. Unlike Karrine "Superhead" Steffans, Kim lures her people in and makes sure they come out of the deal with just as much as she does. She could have been on some slick shit and secretly taped Ray J in the sex tape they made together. That's not what she did. She convinced him that making the movie would be a powerful move for the both of them, and it was. They both got millions of dollars worth of free publicity, which in turn blew them both up larger than life.

Ray J was always known as the R&B star Brandy's little brother and Kim was known as Robert Kardashian's daughter (Robert Kardashian is one of the men that worked on the amazing legal team that exonerated OJ Simpson from the murder of his ex-wife and Kim's mother's friend, Nicole Simpson). Kim and Ray got paid from the sales of the video, but that was just a stepping stone compared to her next move. She landed a deal with a cable network that not only helped her to build her brand but made her millions of dollars.

Everyone tuned into *The Kardashians* and she used the show

to sell her products and make herself larger than life. There was one episode where she charged millions to witness her wedding with NBA star Chris Humphries, only to divorce him months later. What was so cold about the show was that it portrayed her square ass family to be good American rich people while she paraded around as the new Marilyn Monroe sex symbol. She used the show to start many other businesses including launching her fragrance, clothing stores and other spin off shows from *The Kardashians*. She is a master at the game and doesn't give a fuck who likes her. She plots and plans her every move and she knows how to attract what she wants. Her moves were so player that even Ray J benefitted from them and has his own show.

One of her slickest moves to me was when she got with Kanye West. She knew that Kanye was the right hand man to the King, that's right King Hov. Jay-Z is married to the Queen, Beyoncé, and they are considered Hip Hop royalty. Kim is smart enough to know that she will never be a Beyoncé, but if she can get next to Kanye, she would be in there. Once she and Kanye got together, you started to see the four of them everywhere. Every time Beyoncé and Jay-Z move, the press follows and they're not going to talk about them without talking about Kim and Kanye. These are great marketing strategies. Here she is looked at as a freak, but on the same stage as Beyoncé and making her brand a household name.

I read that Kim doesn't do shit unless she has a publicist on it and she's making big money. Shit, Beyoncé said they have to pay her too. So when news of the wedding started buzzing, there were reports that Kim was going to make millions for the wedding. Allegedly Beyoncé wanted some of that money and was turned down. Jay and Bey didn't make the festivities that day.

In the hood, we see chicks fucking everybody for free and we see porn stars do sets for anywhere from $1K and up and that's cool. But Kim made one chess move and now she's worth over $10M. Not bad for someone who got freaky for a day. When Steve Harvey wrote the book *Think Like A Man Act Like A Woman*, he was talking about Kim. She is a constant manipulator and if you enter into her web, she will deceive you. She plans way down the road and if you're not smooth, you will get caught up in her plot. Look at her moves. It is plain as daylight that she strategizes each move down to the last one.

THE BREAKDOWN

The real-life examples in this chapter can be used as a guide on what to do in any situation. You must prevail at all times in order to win, and stumbling with solutions at the last minute will ensure a loss. Master the moves that were made by the greatest human chess players of all time and you will be able to better maneuver in life. Think strategically and rationally to yield the best results.

Study the power moves in this chapter. The above mentioned names are all seriously playing this game better than anyone in the world. They have been able to outfox and crush every opponent that has attempted to challenge them. This is the goal. Believe that in our lifetime, people will try us on a regular basis. If you keep your mind on your money and focus on succeeding, you will always advance in life. Focusing on anything that does not assist you in moving forward and adding positives in your life only decreases your value as a human chess player. Keep it real with yourself and make boss moves only from this point on. If you are ever in a situation where you are unsure of a decision to make, refer to *The Art of Human Chess: A Study Guide to Winning.*

Chess Notes

Final Note

Contact Pimpin' Ken for interviews,
albums, shows or speaking engagements:

414.399.3611

Instagram: @realpimpken

Twitter: @therealpimpken

Facebook/PimpinKenBook

www.pimpinken.net

theartofhumanchess7@gmail.com

theartofhumanchess7@yahoo.com

"Don't stay in bed unless you can make money in bed."
~George Burns~

Although this book was written to enlighten you, there is still a lot of work left for you down the road. My learning about the connection between human chess and the game of chess in the joint may have helped me in my endeavors in life but it's the many books that I have read that have helped me along the way to make better decisions and strategize power moves. *Think and Grow Rich* by Napoleon Hill, *The 48 Laws of Power* by Robert Greene, *The Art of War* by Sun Tzu, *The Autobiography of Malcolm X* as told to Alex Haley, and *The Art of the Deal* by Donald Trump have been some of the books that have inspired me. You have to use the tools that you have learned in this book such as tactics, strategies, deception, maneuvering and extreme patience to guide you on your journey to becoming a masterful human chess player. Make sure you use them with precision and great focus because your opponent will be using whatever game he or she has to annihilate your ass.

As a master of human chess, I use this book as a chess game within itself to educate my readers about psychology, business, politics and history. This book gives you an alternative way to look at life and shows you that the game you could run for little money is the same game that the politicians, corporate executives and entertainers run for millions. The difference is that the individuals in our society that succeed aim higher than those that do not succeed.

It does not matter if you are rich or poor or Black or White. If you master the information in this book, you will be a force to be reckoned with. Always remember that whether you want to play the game of human chess or not, you're still in it and someone may be trying to play you. You have already armed yourself with this book and now it is time to defend yourself and checkmate your opponent.

Navigate to www.pimpinken.net and continue to learn. Also

follow me on Instagram @realpimpken for daily inspiration.

Chessionary

Baller – a nigga with money

Bid –prison sentence, usually at least a year or more

Blade – a street where hos work (also track)

Bottom Bitch – a pimp's main ho, the one who rides in the front seat

Conman – someone who lies to get money

Game – street knowledge or knowledge about a particular thing that other people don't have

Green – inexperienced in the game

Hater – someone who dislikes or is jealous of another person without merit

Ho – a promiscuous person or a prostitute who sells her body on the streets

Homeboy – someone who is from the same neighborhood and is considered a friend

Hood – an urban area where street people are located

Joint – prison

Knock – to take the next man's girl

Lay Low – to be low-key and stay out of the way until the appropriate time

Lowkey – a person who doesn't want to be seen and stays off the radar

Mission – send someone astray in a different direction

OG – original gangster or older gentleman that has been around a long time and can teach the younger dudes something

P – pimp

Peep – to be aware of something

Pull My Coat – to wake someone up and put them on game

Renegade – a ho on the track, despite not having a pimp
Slipping – not paying attention
Square – someone who is a "regular" person, not a pimp
Track – a blade
Trick – a customer or date
Trim – to take someone for a loop, to con, to swindle
Twisted – to be confused

VIPs

Pimp C (RIP)
E-40
Too $hort
P. Diddy
Dr. Dre
50 Cent
Troy Ave
Tupac (RIP)
Aaliyah (RIP)
Left Eye (RIP)
Missy Elliott

French Montana
Machine Gun Kelly
Kevin Gates
Big Sean
Akon
Future
Shy Glizzy
The Game
Chris Brown
Jeremih
Usher
Maclemore

Eminem
'Lil Durk
Yo Gotti
'Lil Boosie
'Lil Wayne
Baby
Drake
Nicki Minaj
Jay-Z
Beyoncé
Kanye West
Kim Kardashian

Khloe Kardashian
Kourtney Kardashian
Rhianna
Juicy J
J Cole
Dave Mays
Damon Dash
Young Jeezy
YG
Swizz Beatz
Alicia Keys
Trina

Nelly
Cedric *"The Entertainer"*
Kevin Hart
Steve Harvey
Neyo
Denzel Washington
Will Smith
Ice Cube
Mike Epps
Clifton Powell
Fabolous

Rick Ross
Meek Mills
Wale
Rich Homie Quan
Kendrick Lamar
Young Thug
Tyga
Big Boi
Justin Bieber
Usher
Patti LaBelle
Da Brat

Brandi

Ray J

Benzino

Kim Kardashian

Rev Run

Russell Simmons

Solange

Meagan Good

Christina Aguilera

Eva

Lisa Raye

Terrance Howard

Taraji P. Henson
Nikki Turner
Roxy Reynolds
Chris Brown
Omarion
Benzino
Young Buck
Tony Yayo
Lloyd Banks
Trey Songz
The Core DJs
Tony Neal

DJ Mustard
LA Leakers
'Lil Bankhead
DJ J Nicks
Big Tigger
Grand Master Flash
DJ Red Alert
Jam Master J (RIP)
DJ Premier
Bigga Rakin
DJ Jazzy Jeff
Don Cannon

DJ Kool Herc
Homer Blow
Reggie Brown
Funk Master Flex
DJ Khalid
Pharrell
Timbaland
K Slay
Greg Street
Ron Campbell
Frank Skee
Angela E.

DJ J. Mix
Angie Martinez
Paul Rosenberg
DJ Funky
Shalamar
Morehouse
Spellman
Harvard
Yale
Princeton
Elkhorn
Alabama State

Alverno College
Howard
Marquette
UW-Milwaukee
ILP Video
Worldstar Hip Hop
Hood Box Office
All Hip Hop
XXL
Sister Sister
Hip Hop Weekly
Jet

VIBE
BET
MTV
VH-1
OWN
Clear Channel
Source Magazine
VLAD TV
Big Al
Steve-O
Wise P
Touch the P

Young Rick
Big Silk
Reality
Dopeman
Rayon Payne
Timmy
Jason
King Cam
Marvin
Dreez
Rob "The Eagle"
Owens

Pat Hergins
Rob Dyrdek
Big
Greg Lutzka
Chuck Deal
Sky High
Aaron Polanski
Producer Meech
Rico Love
William Louis
Jonathan, MA Ed
Harrison

Total Entertainment Network
Jayroll
Frog
Timmy
King Mitch
Sonny
Pastor Gill
Christ
Magic City
Onyx
Strokers

'Lil Kenny
KP
Cala
Keke
Ladybug
Ashlynn
Alex
EO
Louis (RIP)
Susan
Mike

Mentors

Father Devine
Pimpin' Poke
Rob Roberson
Tommy Dixon
Sonny Page
Brian Jordan, AKA BJ
Jim Dandy
Greasy
Sluggo
Memphis Jake

Acknowledgements

I owe my thanks to the game and to the people who made it possible for me to put this together. First I'd like to thank my mother and father, Juanita and Collie "Johnnie Slick" Ivy (RIP), who gave me life. My five children: Takiyah Ivy, Kenneth Ajani Ivy, Jr., Cala Reed, Kenneth Supreme Ivy, Jr., Kendriona Ivy AKA Ladybug. My grandbaby: Kennedy Ivy. To Kenisha Briggs, Javonte Briggs and Kenyetta Briggs. My brothers and sisters: Rosemary, Theresa, Collie, Tony (keep your head up, boy, in the joint), Marvin, Elijah (RIP), Lynette, and Evelyn. Special thanks to my editor William Louis Jonathan, MA Ed. To Louis Owens (RIP), Susan Owens, Rob Owens, Ashlynn Adams, Alexandria Owens, William Louis Jonathan, MA Ed, Michael Owens and EA Owens. To my photographer: Harrison D. Kern (Total Entertainment Network). To my nieces and nephews: Jessie, Sherise, Chris, Andrenna, Taurus, Renee, Dominique, Lamontre, Kentwan, Zaresha, Marajsha, Antroness, Cortez, Anisha, Tekeda, Lakeya, Tyquesha, Shatorya. My cousins Reggie, Tywanda, Lester, Victor, Ricky, Danny, Al (RIP), Sheila, Zelma, and Nuke. To Linda, Regina, Tanya, and Mark, and all y'all down there in Oxford, Mississippi. To all the folks from Milwaukee who ever walked the Earth with me: JD AKA Father Divine Rob Roberson, Tommy Dixon, John Brown (RIP), Sonny Paige (RIP), Bobby Hill, Sammy, Memphis AKA Tick Tock, BJ (RIP), Petey Paige, Brandy (RIP), Flip AKA June Bug (RIP), Marty Freeman (RIP), Grit, K-Mack, Little Daddy, CC, Twan, Mr. Terry, Pimp Little, Mick, John Carter, Pimpin' Paul, Hollywood, King Gus, Pimp Ike, Old Man Pimpin' Ike (RIP), Lefty, Kemp, Kurt Blow, Ronny Jewel, Slim, Elroy (RIP), Pimpin' T-Bone, Greg Farmer, Little Rob, Pimpin' Sam, Pimpin' Scoob, the Great Poke, Funtaine, Johnny Goodlow (RIP), Triple D, Superb, Twonyae (RIP), Dorele, Sluggo, Big B, Chicago, Gene, Willie D, Kickin' It Jack, Thomas, Old Man Running Bear, Milwaukee Buck, my cousin Greasy, Sackson, Mack the Knife, Julius Nash, Kool in Dickie, Sonny Carter, Baby Love, Chris Soloman, Memphis Jake, Esquire, Billy Bugs, Melvin Grant and the Grant family, Ted Beamon, Mike Beamon, Ray Lynn, Dae Dae, Priest, Karl Sloan and the Sloan family, Pimpin' Stand, Chris Taylor, Walbash, Sport, CB, Boo Boo, Brian Ivory, Leroy Bell, E-Noble, Frankie Fox, Jay Fox, Sport (AC), J Rock, Young CB, Danny Tubs, Michael Tubs, and for all my other friends out of Milwaukee that I didn't mention—I have not forgotten y'all! To: Frog, Elliot, Poppa Quin, Eastside Quawn, Jim Dandy, Pee Wee Ferguson, Brian Ferguson, John Ferguson and the Ferguson family, Seahorse, Reggie, my brother from another mother Porter Magee, Big K, Buzzer James, Don, Mike Banks, Greg Bradford, Greg Groves, Little Greg, C Money, Leonard Ross, the Eastside homies, KG, Tree, Chris Davis (RIP), Doo Doo, Baby Drew, Big Kurt, Marvell, Little June (RIP), Elliot (RIP), Mario (RIP), Earl the Pearl, La La, Parish, L.A., Corey, Baby Dad, Big Tone, Bohannon, Twan, Dawan, Stacy, Bruce, Mick, Rob, Little Corey (on the beats), Short Mack, Comossie, Porgie, Smoke, Charlie Mack, Perry, Toot, The Twins, Black D, Action Blue, Oily Mike, JD (RIP), Scottie AKA SB, Sam, Harvey, Richie, and Angel. To some more of my player friends: Cash Ball, Young Twan, Young'un, CooCoo Cal, Ralph, Smalls, Smitty Darbie, Steve Snowball, 2-4 Tweet (RIP), 2-4 RC (RIP), Germ, Pig, Precious, Arby, Money Mike, Reesco, Teddy AKA Tim. To all my international friends: Suave, Young Rick, Napoleon, Skinny, Daytona D, Valentino, JuJu, King Burt, King James, Brink, King Boo (RIP), Good Game, Reverend Seamore, Bishop Don Magic Juan, Scooter G, Ronny Slim, Avalanche, Candy, Little Candy, Love, GA (Game Affiliated), Be Rich, Jap, Mackie, Bobby, RP, Kansas City's Finest, Gorgeous Dre, Fast, Gangsta Brown, Fillmore Slim, DC Buttons, Bubblicious, Pimp CC from California, Antwan, Mr. Bolden, Big Silk, Spec Spectacular, Shorty P, Ross from Cleveland, Godfather, Cash from ATL, Revenue, Charm, Reverend Toby, Vic Mighty Brown, Brick from the West Side of Chicago, Mike, Burroughs, Scorpio, King Bean (RIP), Slick Vic, Atlanta Red, Little D, J Mitch, Israel, D from Nashville, Tim and Terrell from Nashville, Cool Ace, Sheep Dog, Will, Alex from Mississippi, Bobby Brome, Pocket Knife (RIP), Dooby from LA, Segel, Lynch-Bay, Cornell, Christ, Goldie McDowell, T' Rom Nashville, California Mike, Succeed, Memphis Black, Success, Blue Diamond, Supreme, Smiley, International Red, Mack Slim, Little Ronny Slim, Mr. Tate, Payday, Mack Dre, King Cam. To all my friends in Hip Hop who helped me come up: Pimp C (RIP), Too Short, Juvenile, J Reezy from Detroit Cartel, 50 Cent, Mack 10, Pastor Troy, Project Pat, 'Lil Jon, Trillville, 'Lil Scrappy, Slim Thug, Mike Jones, Young Jeezy, Chamillionaire, Jermaine Dupri, Nelly, P. Diddy, Loom, Reality from FUP Mob, Stackin Cheese, David Banner, 'Lil Flip, Red Eyes, Baby and 'Lil Wayne from Cash Money Records, Young Boss, Outkast, Snoop Dogg, U Dig Records, Fabolous, Raekwon, Nick Cannon, Fat Man Scoop, Ed Lover, K Slay, Young Buck, Greg Street, Frank Ski. To Alverno College, Howard, Harvard, Yale, Princeton. To Source magazine, F.E.D.S. magazine, Vibe magazine, XXL magazine, Street magazine, Scarface, Young Bleed, Comedian Shorty, Comedian Davole, Da Brat, Gangster Boo, Boo and Gottie, 112, Jagged Edge, Usher, E-40, Skip and Waco from UTP, Biz Markie, 'Lil Bow Wow, Ice-T, Lloyd Banks, C-Bone, Skim, Steve Harvey, Cedric the Entertainer, Big Mike, Gip, Ali, C-Lo , C-Bo (Goodie Mob), Show Time, Third, Decatur Black, Player Puncho, Rico Love, DJ Funky, Tony Neal, Homer Blow, DJ Don, Reggie Brown, Core DJs, Kid Capri, Mike Pratt, DJ Dimp, Mommy True La, Jazzy Pha, Nitty, Shorty Red, Faybo, Dem Franchise Boys, Ying Yang Twins, 8-Ball, MJG, Magic from Magic City, Casper, Stainless Entertainment, Young City Chopper, T-Gray, Archie Lee, E from the Outsiders, Kembre Track Boys, St. Lunatics, Keywan, Murphy Lee, Danny Christian, Benny Boon, David Palmer, Chris Robertson, Chingy, DeShay Jones from D Productions, Tinandre Johnson, Genari Fitzgerald, Gemari Fitzgerald, JuJuan Blunt, Rosalyn Brown-Blunt, Justin Blunt, Shearl Davis, Sherica Knox, London Knox, Arnitta Holliman, To my Moor brother: Too Sweet, 'Lil Boosie and 'Lil Webby, Dub C, Dru Down, C Note, The Game, Nas, Jadakiss, Whodini, and many, many more. Last thanks to Dopeman from ChronicCentral.net, Terrel from Morgan Designs, C-Money from No Nonsense, Marvin Ivy from Ivy-Media, Jayroll from Dying Breed Music, Steve-O from Infinite Records, Debbie the Glass Lady, Allston, Terrel from Shoot 2 Films, Jay Dog from Selective Hits Distribution, Carla from Dallas, Donald Jet, B-Dog, Avie the Pimp, Ed from Nashville, 'Lil Farrakan from Milwaukee, Chug, Pokie, Poonie, Ren, Big Meech from BMF, Fiskani, and George Kareem out of Atlanta.

Coming Soon from Author Pimpin' Ken:

I. **Pimp and Grow Rich**
II. **The Gambler**
III. **Inside a Pimp's Stable**
IV. **Rich Pimp, Poor Pimp**
V. **The Autobiography of Pimpin' Ken: Pimp, Not the Story of My Life**

Printed in Great Britain
by Amazon

47691313R00128